Ninja Blender Cookbook for Beginners

365 Days of Ninja Blender Recipes, Juicing for Your Family's Well-being, Boost Energy, Lose Weight Fast, Detoxify, Burn Fat, Rejuvenate and Feel Years Younger!

Adalys Hartington

Table of Contents

INTRODUCTION

The Health Benefits Of Smoothies

Smoothies offer a plethora of health benefits, making them a popular and nutritious choice for individuals seeking a convenient and tasty way to enhance their well-being. As you explore the diverse recipes for your Ninja Blender, it's worth delving into the numerous advantages that smoothies can bring to your overall health.

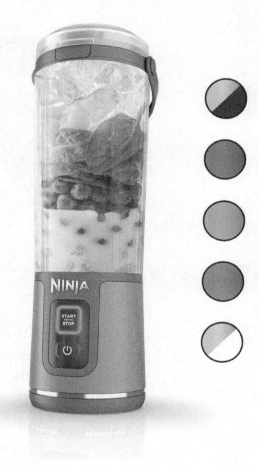

- Nutrient-Packed Powerhouses:

  One of the primary benefits of smoothies is their ability to pack a nutritional punch. By blending various fruits, vegetables, and other wholesome ingredients, you can create a beverage that contains a rich array of essential vita Mins, minerals, and antioxidants. These nutrients play crucial roles in supporting various bodily functions, including immune system function, skin health, and energy metabolism.

- Weight Management and Satiety:

  Smoothies can be a valuable ally in weight management. Incorporating fiber-rich ingredients such as fruits, vegetables, and seeds into your smoothies promotes a feeling of fullness, potentially reducing overall

calorie intake throughout the day. Additionally, the combination of fiber and liquid in smoothies can contribute to better digestion and regular bowel movements, supporting a healthy gastrointestinal system.

- Hydration Boost:

    Staying hydrated is vital for overall health, and smoothies can contribute to your daily fluid intake. While water is essential, incorporating hydrating fruits like watermelon, cucumber, or berries into your smoothies adds flavor and additional hydration benefits. This is especially beneficial for those who struggle to meet their daily water intake goals.

- Versatile Protein Sources:

    Protein is a crucial macronutrient that plays a key role in muscle repair, immune function, and overall body maintenance. Your Ninja Blender

allows you to easily incorporate various protein sources into your smoothies, such as Greek yogurt, nut butters, seeds, or protein powder. Including protein in your smoothies can contribute to muscle preservation and help keep you feeling satisfied for longer periods.

- Enhanced Nutrient Absorption:

Blending ingredients in a smoothie breaks down cell walls and fibers, making the nutrients more easily absorbed by the body. This process, known as pre-digestion, can enhance the bioavailability of nutrients, ensuring that your body can efficiently utilize the vita Mins and minerals present in the ingredients.

- Blood Sugar Regulation:

For individuals managing their blood sugar levels, smoothies can be a convenient and delicious way to incorporate low-glycemic fruits and vegetables. The fiber and protein content in smoothies can contribute to more stable blood sugar levels, preventing rapid spikes and crashes.

- Convenient and Time-Saving:

    In today's fast-paced world, convenience is key. The Ninja Blender's portability and ease of use make it convenient to whip up a nutritious smoothie in a matter of minutes. This can be especially beneficial for those with busy schedules, providing a quick and accessible option for a healthy meal or snack.

In conclusion, the health benefits of smoothies are diverse and impactful. From providing a concentrated source of essential nutrients to supporting weight management and hydration, incorporating smoothies into your diet can contribute to a holistic approach to well-being. With your Ninja Blender and its versatile features, you have the tools to explore a wide range of smoothie recipes that cater to your taste preferences and health goals.

Why You Should Make Them At Home

Store-bought smoothies may seem like a convenient option, but they often come with a set of drawbacks that can impact your health negatively. Making your smoothies at home with a Ninja Blender provides a healthier alternative for several reasons.

- Hidden Sugars and Artificial Additives:

    Many store-bought smoothies are loaded with hidden sugars and artificial additives. These can include high-fructose corn syrup, artificial sweeteners, and preservatives. Excessive sugar consumption has been linked to various health issues such as obesity, diabetes, and heart disease. When you make smoothies at home, you have control over the ingredients, allowing you to choose natural sweeteners and avoid unnecessary additives.

- Lack of Fresh Ingredients:

    Store-bought smoothies may not prioritize the use of fresh, whole ingredients. Instead, they might rely on fruit concentrates and purees which can lack the nutritional value of fresh fruits and vegetables. Using a Ninja Blender at home allows you to include a variety of fresh and nutrient-rich ingredients, ensuring that your smoothie is packed with vita Mins, minerals, and antioxidants.

- Customization for Dietary Needs:

    Homemade smoothies offer the flexibility to tailor the ingredients to meet your specific dietary needs. Whether you follow a particular diet such as keto, paleo, or have allergies, making your smoothies at home allows

you to control the ingredients, ensuring they align with your nutritional requirements.

- Portion Control:

Store-bought smoothies often come in larger sizes, contributing to overconsumption of calories. With the Ninja Blender's 18 oz. capacity, you can control portion sizes more effectively. This is particularly beneficial if you're mindful of your calorie intake or trying to manage your weight.

- Freshness and Nutrient Retention:

The process of mass-producing and distributing store-bought smoothies can lead to a loss of freshness and nutrient degradation. Making smoothies at home with the Ninja Blender ensures that you consume your beverage immediately after blending, preserving the maximum amount of nutrients and flavors from the ingredients.

- Cost-Effectiveness:

  While store-bought smoothies might seem like a convenient option, they can be expensive in the long run. Investing in a Ninja Blender and preparing your smoothies at home allows you to save money while enjoying the freshest and healthiest ingredients.

- Hygiene and Cleanliness:

  The ease of cleaning the Ninja Blender, with its BPA-free and dishwasher-safe lid and vessel, promotes good hygiene. Store-bought smoothies, on the other hand, involve single-use containers that contribute to environmental waste and may not always be cleaned thoroughly during the manufacturing process.

In conclusion, the Ninja Blender offers a convenient and healthy solution for making smoothies at home. By taking control of the ingredients, you can ensure that your smoothies are free from hidden sugars, artificial additives, and other unhealthy components commonly found in store-bought alternatives. Making your smoothies with the Ninja Blender not only promotes better health but also allows for customization, portion control, and cost-effectiveness. Embracing the practice of preparing homemade smoothies is a step towards a healthier lifestyle.

How To Use Your Usb Blender

Using your Ninja USB Blender is a breeze, and you'll be whipping up delicious smoothies and blends in no time. Here's a comprehensive guide to help you make the most of this portable blending powerhouse.

- Charging the Blender:

  Before you start, ensure that your USB blender is fully charged. Use the provided USB-C cable to connect the blender to a power source. The rechargeable 7.4V power base is convenient and allows you to blend without being tethered to an outlet.

- Assembling the Blender:

  Attach the blending vessel to the motor base. Ensure it's securely in place to prevent any mishaps during blending. The vessel features a ribbed design for optimal blending performance.

- Adding Ingredients:

  Prepare your favorite ingredients for blending. Whether it's fruits, vegetables, or frozen items, the Ninja Blender with Blast Technology can handle them all. The durable, stainless steel BlastBlade Assembly is

designed to crush ice and handle frozen ingredients with ease.

- Power and Blend Buttons:

Familiarize yourself with the separate power and blend buttons. This feature prevents unintentional blending, allowing you to power on the device before engaging the blades. Press the power button first, then the blend button when you're ready to start blending.

- Blending Process:

With the buttons pressed, watch as the ribbed vessel creates a vortex, pulling the ingredients towards the powerful BlastBlade Assembly. The Ninja Blast Technology ensures a smooth and consistent blend every time.

- Sip Lid Usage:

Once your blend is ready, use the easy-open sip lid to transform your

blending vessel into a convenient to-go cup. The lid is designed for comfortable sipping while on the move. The carrying handle adds to the portability, making it easy to take your drinks wherever you go.

- Cleaning Your Blender:

  After enjoying your delicious blend, cleaning is a breeze. The lid and vessel are BPA-free and dishwasher safe, ensuring a hygienic cleaning process. Additionally, the blender can self-clean with a 30-second blend cycle using water and a drop of dish soap. This feature saves time and makes cleanup hassle-free.

- Recipe Inspiration Guide:

  Explore the 5-recipe Inspiration Guide included in the Quick Start Guide and Instruction Booklet. This guide offers creative ideas to expand your blending repertoire. From refreshing fruit smoothies to nutrient-packed green blends, there's a recipe for every taste.

- Troubleshooting Tips:

In case you encounter any issues, refer to the Instruction Booklet for troubleshooting tips. Whether it's about charging, blending consistency, or maintenance, the booklet provides valuable insights to keep your Ninja Blender running smoothly.

- Enjoying the Portable Freedom:

    One of the key advantages of the USB blender is its portability. Take advantage of the cordless operation and USB-C compatibility to blend drinks anywhere you go. Whether you're at the office, the gym, or on a hiking trail, your Ninja Blender is ready to serve up refreshing beverages.

In conclusion, the Ninja USB Blender offers a seamless blending experience with its rechargeable power base, durable design, and user-friendly features. By following these steps, you'll unlock the full potential of your blender and enjoy the convenience of on-the-go blending. Cheers to a healthier and tastier lifestyle!

Why You Need This Book

The recipe book for the Ninja Blender serves as an essential companion for anyone seeking a seamless blending experience that transcends the boundaries of traditional kitchen setups. Its significance lies in the diverse range of recipes and creative concoctions it offers, tailored to harness the full potential of the Ninja Blender's cutting-edge features.

First and foremost, the book becomes a culinary ally for those who crave convenience without compromising on taste or nutrition. The portable blending power of the Ninja Blender allows users to effortlessly create smooth and nutritious drinks on the go. Whether you are a fitness enthusiast in need of a post-workout protein shake or a busy professional seeking a quick, wholesome breakfast option, this recipe book caters to your time-sensitive lifestyle.

The large capacity of the blender, producing up to 18 oz. of your favorite blends, further emphasizes its suitability for various occasions. The recipe book takes full advantage of this capacity, presenting a plethora of recipes for everything from refreshing fruit smoothies to indulgent frozen desserts. With the Ninja Blender and this book in hand, you can easily cater to both personal cravings and entertaining guests with impressive, flavorful concoctions.

The premium colors available for the blender add a touch of personalization to your blending experience. The recipe book aligns with this aspect by offering recipes that not only tantalize your taste buds but also complement your style preferences. Whether you opt for a vibrant tropical smoothie or a rich, decadent chocolate shake, the book ensures that your blending experience is not only

gastronomically satisfying but visually appealing as well.

The easy-to-carry design, complete with a comfortable hinged carry handle, transforms the Ninja Blender into a travel-friendly culinary companion. The recipe book recognizes the blender's portability and crafts recipes suitable for picnics, road trips, or simply enjoying a refreshing beverage during your daily commute. The integration of the sip lid, allowing users to blend and drink from the same vessel, further enhances the convenience of enjoying your favorite blends wherever you are.

Maintaining hygiene and ensuring effortless cleanup is a priority in any kitchen. The book complements the Ninja Blender's easy-to-clean design, where both the lid and vessel are BPA-free and dishwasher safe. Moreover, the blender's self-cleaning capability with a 30-second blend cycle using water and a drop of dish soap aligns with the book's emphasis on simplicity and cleanliness.

The innovative Ninja Blast Technology, featuring a ribbed vessel and durable stainless steel BlastBlade Assembly, is a testament to the blender's prowess in handling various ingredients, including ice and frozen elements. The recipe book maximizes the potential of this technology by offering recipes that capitalize on the blender's ability to create a vortex, ensuring consistently smooth and well-blended results.

The separation of power and blend buttons addresses a common concern of unintentional blending, adding an extra layer of safety and control to the blending process. The book, in turn, aligns with this feature by providing clear instructions and recipes that guide users through each step, minimizing the chances of mishaps.

The inclusion of a rechargeable power base, operating at 7.4 V and compatible with USB-C, enhances the blender's versatility. The recipe book incorporates this feature by presenting recipes that cater to both indoor and outdoor settings, ensuring that you can enjoy your favorite blends without the constraints of a power outlet.

In summary, the recipe book for the Ninja Blender becomes an indispensable asset for those who seek a harmonious blend of convenience, versatility, and culinary creativity. By aligning with the blender's features and capabilities, this book elevates your blending experience, making it a seamless and enjoyable part of your daily routine. Whether you are a health-conscious individual, a culinary enthusiast, or someone with a busy lifestyle, the Ninja Blender and its accompanying recipe book offer a delightful fusion of functionality and flavor.

How To Clean A Blender The Easy Way

Cleaning your Ninja Blender is a breeze with its user-friendly design and materials. Follow these simple steps to ensure your blender stays in top condition while maintaining the convenience of easy cleaning.

- Immediate Rinse: After using your Ninja Blender, it's advisable to rinse the blending vessel immediately. This prevents any residue from drying and becoming harder to clean later. For a quick rinse, add warm water and a drop of dish soap to the vessel, then run a short blending cycle.

- Disassembly: Before proceeding with a more thorough cleaning, make sure to disassemble the blender components. Detach the blending vessel from the power base and remove the lid, sip lid, and the stainless steel BlastBlade Assembly. This step allows for easier access to all parts of the blender.

- Hand Wash or Dishwasher: The lid and blending vessel of your Ninja Blender are BPA-free and dishwasher safe. Simply place them on the top rack of your dishwasher for a convenient cleanup. Alternatively, you can hand wash the components using warm, soapy water and a non-abrasive sponge.

- Self-Cleaning Function: Take advantage of the self-cleaning feature of your Ninja Blender. Fill the blending vessel halfway with warm water, add a drop of dish soap, and reassemble the blender. Run a 30-second blend cycle to let the self-cleaning function do its work. This is a quick and efficient way to handle light residue.

- Blade Cleaning: Pay special attention to the stainless steel BlastBlade Assembly. To clean it thoroughly, disassemble the blades from the base carefully. Be cautious while handling the sharp blades. Wash them separately under running water or in the dishwasher. A small brush can

help reach tight spaces and ensure a meticulous cleaning.

- Base Wipe-down: Since the power base is rechargeable and contains electronic components, avoid submerging it in water. Instead, use a damp cloth to wipe down the base, ensuring no food residue is left on the surface. Be mindful not to let any water seep into the electronic components.
- USB-C Cable: The USB-C cable, being an essential part of the blender's rechargeable feature, should not be overlooked. Wipe it down with a damp cloth if needed, ensuring there is no food residue on the cable.
- Regular Maintenance: To keep your Ninja Blender in top-notch condition, make cleaning a regular part of your routine. This ensures that no stubborn residues accumulate over time, making the cleaning process more manageable and preserving the longevity of your blender.

By following these easy steps, you'll maintain the cleanliness of your Ninja Blender effortlessly. Regular cleaning not only ensures hygiene but also contributes to the longevity and optimal performance of your blender, allowing you to enjoy smooth and delicious blends every time.

Chapter 1: Fruit Smoothies

Strawberry Cashew Smoothie

Prep Time: 4 Hrs   Cook Time: 10 Mins   Serves: 2

Ingredients:

- 1/3 cup unsalted cashews, soaked
- 1 1/2 cups frozen strawberries
- 1 1/2 cups frozen cauliflower
- 1 1/2 cups cashew milk
- 2 tablespoons hemp hearts
- 2 tablespoons honey
- 1 tablespoon chia seeds
- 1 teaspoon bee pollen plus extra for sprinkle
- 1 teaspoon vanilla extract
- 1/8 teaspoon sea salt

Directions:

1. Add all the ingredients to a Ninja blender and blend until creamy and smooth.
2. Pour into glasses, top with bee pollen and serve!

Nutritional Value (Amount per Serving):

Calories: 544; Fat: 29.07; Carb: 62.53; Protein: 15.99

Easy Blackberry Smoothie

Prep Time: 5 Mins   Cook Time: 5 Mins   Serves: 1

Ingredients:

- 1 cup frozen blackberries
- 1/2 banana, frozen
- 1/2 cup Greek yogurt
- 1/2 cup almond milk
- 1 tablespoon chia seeds
- 1 tablespoon hemp hearts
- 1 tablespoon ground flax seeds
- 1 tablespoon maple syrup

Directions:

1. Combine all ingredients in a Ninja blender and blend until smooth.
2. Pour into a glass and serve.

Nutritional Value (Amount per Serving):

Calories: 678; Fat: 15.51; Carb: 125.33; Protein: 22.11

Pumpkin Banana Smoothie

Prep Time: 5 Mins   Cook Time: 5 Mins   Serves: 1

Ingredients:

- 1 frozen banana
- 1/2 cup pumpkin puree
- 1/2 cup plain yogurt
- 1/4 cup unsweetened almond milk
- 1/4 teaspoon pumpkin pie spice
- 1 tablespoon maple syrup, optional

Directions:

1. Place all ingredients in blender and blend until smooth and creamy.
2. Pour into a glass, dust with extra pumpkin pie spice and enjoy!

Nutritional Value (Amount per Serving):

Calories: 843; Fat: 35.54; Carb: 121.98; Protein: 26.16

Ingredient Mango Pineapple Smoothie

Prep Time: 5 Mins   Cook Time: 5 Mins   Serves: 1

Ingredients:

- 1 cup frozen mango chunks
- 1 cup frozen pineapple chunks
- 1/2 cup plain yogurt
- 3/4 cup water
- juice of 1/2 a lime, optional
- collagen or protein powder, optional

Directions:

1. Combine all the ingredients in a Ninja blender and blend until smooth and creamy.
2. Pour into a glass and enjoy!

Nutritional Value (Amount per Serving):

Calories: 502; Fat: 20.88; Carb:92.92; Protein: 20.88

Layered Strawberry Ginger Peach Smoothie

Prep Time: 20 Mins   Cook Time: 10 Mins   Serves: 2

Ingredients:

FOR THE STRAWBERRY GINGER LAYER:
- 2 cups whole strawberries, if frozen-thawed, if fresh-hulled
- 1 inch piece fresh ginger, chopped
- splash of orange juice

FOR THE PEACH LAYER:
- 1 cup frozen peach slices
- 1/2 frozen banana
- 1 cup ultra-filtered skim milk, or milk of choice
- 1/2 teaspoon vanilla extract

Directions:

FOR THE STRAWBERRY GINGER LAYER:
1. Combine the strawberries, ginger and orange juice in the blender. Process until a smooth puree.
2. Pour the puree evenly into 2 glasses and place in freezer for 10-15 minutes to set.

FOR THE PEACH LAYER:
1. Rinse out the blender.
2. Combine the peaches, banana, milk and vanilla extract in the blender and blend until smooth.
3. Remove glasses from the freezer and slowly pour the peach layer on top in each glass.
4. Garnish with a mint leaf if desired and serve immediately.

Nutritional Value (Amount per Serving):

Calories: 539; Fat: 10.88; Carb: 100.88; Protein: 17.58

Hydrating Berry Green Smoothie

Prep Time: 5 Mins   Cook Time: 5 Mins   Serves: 1

Ingredients:

- 1 cup frozen strawberries
- 1 cup coconut water
- 6 ounces plain 0% Greek yogurt
- handful baby greens, spinach, kale, etc.
- 1 scoop Herbalife24 CR7 Drive

Directions:

1. Combine all ingredients in a Ninja blender and blend until smooth.

Nutritional Value (Amount per Serving):

Calories: 356; Fat: 6.14; Carb: 55.56; Protein: 22.31

Guava Pineapple Smoothie

Prep Time: 5 Mins   Cook Time: 5 Mins   Serves: 2

Ingredients:

- 4 guavas, about 125g, seeds removed
- 2/3 cup chopped pineapple, about 200g
- 1/2 cup frozen strawberries, about 80g
- 3/4 cup light coconut milk, from a can
- 1/8 teaspoon xanthan gum, optional

Directions:

1. Combine all ingredients in a Ninja blender and blend until smooth.
2. Pour into 2 glasses and serve.

Nutritional Value (Amount per Serving):

Calories: 284; Fat: 21.61; Carb: 24.48; Protein: 2.78

Wild Blueberry Beet Smoothie

Prep Time: 5 Mins   Cook Time: 5 Mins   Serves: 2

Ingredients:

- 1 cup roasted beets
- 1 cup frozen wild blueberries
- 1 cup light canned coconut milk
- 1/2 banana
- 1 serving collagen peptides or 1 serving protein powder
- 1 tablespoon toasted coconut flakes for garnish

Directions:

1. Combine all ingredients except coconut flakes in a Ninja blender. Blend until smooth. Pour into glass and garnish with toasted coconut flakes.

Nutritional Value (Amount per Serving):

Calories: 474; Fat: 26.57; Carb: 56.83; Protein: 9.6

Bubbly Ginger Blood Orange Smoothie

Prep Time: 3 Mins   Cook Time: 5 Mins   Serves: 2

Ingredients:

- 1 blood orange
- 1/4 cup ginger ale, or ginger brew if you have it

- 1/4 cup orange juice
- 1/2 small banana
- 1/4 teaspoon vanilla extract
- dash ground ginger
- handful of ice

Directions:

1. Combine all ingredients in a Ninja blender and blend until smooth.

Nutritional Value (Amount per Serving):

Calories: 160; Fat: 3.82; Carb: 30.05; Protein: 2.22

Pineapple Kiwi Mint Smoothie

Prep Time: 2 Mins   Cook Time: 5 Mins   Serves: 1

Ingredients:

- 1 cup cubed pineapple
- 1 kiwi
- 5-6 mint leaves
- 1/2 cup coconut milk
- 3 ice cubes

Directions:

1. Combine all ingredients in a Ninja blender and blend until smooth.

Nutritional Value (Amount per Serving):

Calories: 632; Fat: 42.87; Carb: 62.34; Protein: 8.79

Persimmon Vanilla Bean Smoothie

Prep Time: 5 Mins   Cook Time: 5 Mins   Serves: 1

Ingredients:

- 1 very ripe Hachiya persimmon, the oblong shaped one rather than the shorter round one
- 1/4 vanilla bean
- 2 tablespoons coconut cream from a can
- 1 cup vanilla almond milk
- 1/8 teaspoon cinnamon
- handful of ice cubes

Directions:

1. Cut the top off of the persimmon and scoop the flesh out into a Ninja blender.

2. Scrape the seeds of the 1/4 vanilla bean out and add into the blender.
3. Add remaining ingredients to blender and blend until smooth.
4. Garnish with extra cinnamon.

Nutritional Value (Amount per Serving):

Calories: 403; Fat: 20.07; Carb: 56.31; Protein: 4.27

Peach Lassi Smoothie

Prep Time: 5 Mins   Cook Time: 5 Mins   Serves: 2

Ingredients:

- 2 peaches, chopped
- 1/2 cup coconut water
- 3/4 cup kefir, or plain greek yogurt*
- 1/2 tablespoon agave
- 1/8 teaspoon cinnamon
- 1/8 teaspoon nutmeg
- 1/8 teaspoon cardamom
- pinch of salt
- 1/2 cup ice

Directions:

1. Combine all ingredients in a Ninja blender and blend until ice is completely pureed, pulsing a few times to break up chunks.
2. Pour into glasses and garnish with pistachios, mint or cardamom on top if desired.

Nutritional Value (Amount per Serving):

Calories: 371; Fat: 11.21; Carb: 69.09; Protein: 4.17

Coconut Lime Smoothie

Prep Time: 5 Mins   Cook Time: 5 Mins   Serves: 2

Ingredients:

- 10 ounces coconut milk from a can
- 5 leaves of mint, plus more for garnish
- 1 tablespoon honey
- 1/4 inch nub of fresh ginger
- juice of 1/2 a lime
- 1/4 cup kefir
- 3/4-1 cup ice

Directions:

1. Combine all ingredients in a Ninja blender and blend until smooth but still icy.
2. Add additional crushed ice to two glasses, pour in drink and garnish with more mint leaves.

Nutritional Value (Amount per Serving):

Calories: 524; Fat: 44.48; Carb: 31.21; Protein: 6.92

Blood Orange Smoothie

Prep Time: 5 Mins   Cook Time: 5 Mins   Serves: 1

Ingredients:

- juice of 1 blood orange
- 1 frozen banana
- 1/2 cup plain greek yogurt, or vanilla ice cream for a dessert smoothie
- 3/4 cup orange juice
- 1 tablespoon blood orange zest
- 1/2 teaspoon vanilla extract
- 1/4 teaspoon ginger
- 2 teaspoons honey or agave
- handful of ice

Directions:

1. Combine all ingredients in a Ninja blender and blend until creamy and smooth.

Nutritional Value (Amount per Serving):

Calories: 777; Fat: 9.64; Carb: 164.38; Protein: 19.73

Chocolate Banana Peanut Butter Smoothie

Prep Time: 5 Mins   Cook Time: 5 Mins   Serves: 2

Ingredients:

- 1 cup of milk, I used 1/2 coconut, 1/2 almond
- 1 frozen banana
- 1 tablespoon unsweetened dark cocoa powder
- 1 individually wrapped dark chocolate square
- 1/3 cup greek yogurt
- 2 tablespoons peanut butter
- handful of ice

Directions:

1. Combine all ingredients in a Ninja blender and blend until smooth and creamy.

Nutritional Value (Amount per Serving):

Calories: 406; Fat: 13.45; Carb: 64.93; Protein: 11.14

Mango Breakfast Smoothie

Prep Time: 5 Mins   Cook Time: 5 Mins   Serves: 1

Ingredients:

- flesh from 1 ripe mango
- 2 cup. plain greek yogurt
- 3 tablespoons oats
- 1 tablespoon chia seeds
- 1 1/2 tablespoons ground flaxseed
- 1 tablespoon agave
- 1/4 cup 1% milk
- handful of ice

Directions:

1. Combine all ingredients in a Ninja blender and puree until smooth.

Nutritional Value (Amount per Serving):

Calories: 589; Fat: 22.72; Carb: 68.29; Protein: 41.6

Coconut Persimmon Smoothie

Prep Time: 5 Mins   Cook Time: 5 Mins   Serves: 1

Ingredients:

- Fruit of 1 very ripe persimmon
- 1 cup coconut milk
- 1/4 teaspoon ginger
- 1/4 teaspoon nutmeg
- 1/2 teaspoon agave
- 1/2 cup ice

Directions:

1. Combine all ingredients in a Ninja blender and blend until smooth.

Nutritional Value (Amount per Serving):

Calories: 870; Fat: 71.44; Carb: 61.11; Protein: 8.91

Pear Smoothie

Prep Time: 5 Mins   Cook Time: 5 Mins   Serves: 1

Ingredients:

- 1 small ripe pear
- 1/2 frozen banana
- 1 scoop vanilla protein powder of choice or collagen peptides
- 1/2 teaspoon cinnamon
- 1/4 teaspoon cardamom
- 1/2 cup almond milk
- 1/2 cup ice
- 1/8 teaspoon xanthan gum, *optional

Directions:

1. Combine all ingredients in a Ninja blender and process until smooth.

Nutritional Value (Amount per Serving):

Calories: 711; Fat: 18.81; Carb: 112.03; Protein: 30.57

Avocado Citrus Smoothie

Prep Time: 5 Mins   Cook Time: 5 Mins   Serves: 1

Ingredients:

- 1/2 avocado
- 1 frozen banana
- 1/4 cup plain yogurt, I used Greek 0%
- juice of half a lemon
- juice of half an orange
- 1/2 teaspoon agave
- 1/2 almond milk
- 1/4 cup water
- pinch of salt

Directions:

1. Combine everything in a Ninja blender and blend until smooth.

Nutritional Value (Amount per Serving):

Calories: 1212; Fat: 57.76; Carb: 177.39; Protein: 19.2

Mango Smoothie

Prep Time: 5 Mins   Cook Time: 5 Mins   Serves: 1

Ingredients:

- 3/4 large mango
- 1/2 cup plain yogurt, I used Greek 0% but, regular plain yogurt will work also
- 1/2 cup milk
- 1/4 cup water
- 1 tablespoon sugar
- pinch of cardamom
- ice

Directions:

1. Combine all ingredients in blender and blend until smooth.

Nutritional Value (Amount per Serving):

Calories: 443; Fat: 15.61; Carb: 69.09; Protein: 13.51

Chapter 2: Green Smoothies

Anti-Inflammatory Green Smoothie

Prep Time: 10 Mins   Cook Time: 5 Mins   Serves: 1

Ingredients:

- 1/4 cup chopped pear, skin on
- 2 teaspoons freshly grated ginger
- 1/4 cup fresh spinach
- 1/4 cup oat milk
- 2 teaspoons hemp or chia seeds
- 1 teaspoon honey or maple syrup (optional)
- 1 cup ice

Directions:

1. In a Ninja blender, add the pear, ginger, spinach, milk, and seeds and blend till smooth.
2. Add 1/2 cup ice and blend till smooth and frothy.
3. Taste and see if it needs a sweetener like honey or maple syrup.

Nutritional Value (Amount per Serving):

Calories: 542; Fat: 31.16; Carb: 59.33; Protein: 12.06

The Best Anti-Inflammatory Smoothie

Prep Time: 5 Mins   Cook Time: 5 Mins   Serves: 1

Ingredients:

- 1 cup unsweetened almond milk
- 1 frozen banana, sliced
- 1/4 inch piece of fresh ginger (peeled and sliced)
- 1/4 inch piece of fresh turmeric (peeled and sliced)
- 1/4 teaspoon ground cinnamon
- 1/2 teaspoon chia seeds
- 1/2 teaspoon flax seeds
- 1 cup fresh baby spinach

Directions:

1. Place all ingredients in the blender and blend for several minutes until very smooth.
2. Pour into a glass and drink up. Enjoy!

Nutritional Value (Amount per Serving):

Calories: 445; Fat: 6.7; Carb: 99.58; Protein: 6.05

Anti-Inflammatory Vegan Green Smoothie

Prep Time: 10 Mins   Cook Time: 5 Mins   Serves: 1-2

Ingredients:

- 1 cup flax milk (or other plant milk)
- 1 cup frozen mango chunks
- 2 cups loosely packed spinach leaves
- 1/2 avocado
- 1/2 large frozen banana
- 1/2 teaspoon cinnamon
- 1/4 teaspoon spirulina powder
- generous pinch of turmeric
- 1 tablespoon chia seeds
- 1/2 teaspoon pure vanilla extract
- 1 tablespoon pure maple syrup
- 1 tablespoon almond butter/sunflower seed butter
- 3-5 tablespoons orange juice

Directions:

1. Add all of the ingredients to your Ninja blender starting with the milk and blend until smooth. I like to add the orange juice at the end, as it helps if the frozen fruit gets stuck, but just add it 1 tablespoon at a time until you achieve the desired smoothie consistency. If it's too thin, add a few more chunks of frozen mango.

Nutritional Value (Amount per Serving):

Calories: 422; Fat: 16.26; Carb: 61.97; Protein: 15.97

Anti-Inflammatory Strawberry Green Smoothie

Prep Time: 5 Mins   Cook Time: 5 Mins   Serves: 1

Ingredients:

- 10 ounces unsweetened almond, coconut, hemp milk or water
- 1 cup frozen organic strawberries
- 1/2 green (unripe) banana
- 1/2 small beet
- 1 large handful kale (de-stemmed), spinach or romaine
- 1 teaspoon unrefined virgin coconut oil
- 1 serving of hemp, collagen or whey protein powder
- 1 tablespoon ground flax seeds* or chia seeds
- 1/2 teaspoon organic vanilla

- Stevia or maple syrup taste (optional)

Directions:

1. Blend all ingredients until smooth.
2. Taste and add sweetener if desired.

Nutritional Value (Amount per Serving):

Calories: 2055; Fat: 157.6; Carb: 109.61; Protein: 84.15

Spinach Prune Smoothie

Prep Time: 5 Mins   Cook Time: 5 Mins   Serves: 1

Ingredients:

- 1 cup ice
- 1/2 cup unsweetened almond milk
- 1/2 cup water
- 1/2 frozen banana
- 1 cup baby spinach or other greens
- 1/4 cup prunes
- 1/2 tablespoon chia seeds
- 1 tablespoon honey or maple syrup

Directions:

1. Put all ingredients into a Ninja blender and blend until smooth.

Nutritional Value (Amount per Serving):

Calories: 720; Fat: 25.47; Carb: 123.13; Protein: 9.45

Strawberry Spinach Smoothie

Prep Time: 5 Mins   Cook Time: 5 Mins   Serves: 2

Ingredients:

- 1/2 cup unsweetened almond milk (or milk of choice)
- 1/4 cup plain non-fat Greek yogurt
- 2 cups baby spinach
- 1/2 cup fresh or frozen strawberries
- 1 frozen banana, broken into chunks
- 1/2 tablespoon honey or maple syrup
- 1/2 teaspoon vanilla extract
- 1/2 cup of ice

Directions:

1. Place all of the ingredients in the blender.

2. Blend until smooth. Serve in two glasses immediately.

Nutritional Value (Amount per Serving):

Calories: 216; Fat: 5.38; Carb: 38.35; Protein: 5.74

Spinach & Cherry Smoothie

Prep Time: 5 Mins   Cook Time: 5 Mins   Serves: 2

Ingredients:

- 1 banana
- 1 cup frozen cherries
- 1 handful spinach
- 1 cup almond milk (or milk of your choice) I use Silk Almond Milk
- 3 ice cubes

Directions:

1. Place all the ingredients in a Ninja blender and process until smooth.

Nutritional Value (Amount per Serving):

Calories: 413; Fat: 7.19; Carb: 85; Protein: 10.07

Almond Cherry Smoothie

Prep Time: 10 Mins   Cook Time: 10 Mins   Serves: 1

Ingredients:

- 1 ripe banana, preferably frozen
- 1 cup frozen cherries (or a cherry and berry mix is great!)
- 2 cups organic spinach (note that this will change the color of the smoothie, but not the flavor)
- 1 tablespoon almond butter
- 1 teaspoon vanilla extract
- 1/4 teaspoon almond extract
- 1/2 cup almond milk (or dairy free milk of choice)

Directions:

1. Add all ingredients to the blender and blend until smooth and creamy.
2. Add more milk if necessary.

Nutritional Value (Amount per Serving):

Calories: 550; Fat: 16.94; Carb: 96.78; Protein: 9.91

Glowing Skin Smoothie

Prep Time: 5 Mins   Cook Time: 5 Mins   Serves: 2

Ingredients:

- 1/2 cup plain coconut water (or more as needed)
- 2 frozen bananas (previously peeled and sliced)
- 1 cup chopped pineapple (frozen or fresh)
- 1 cup chopped mango (frozen or fresh)
- 2 cups spinach or kale
- 1/2 avocado, sliced

Directions:

1. Add all of the ingredients to the blender in the order listed.
2. Blend for at least 3 minutes or until smooth.
3. Add more coconut water if needed to thin out. Scrape down the sides of the blender as needed.

Nutritional Value (Amount per Serving):

Calories: 570; Fat: 9.86; Carb: 128.1; Protein: 7.21

Keto Green Smoothie With Spinach And Avocado

Prep Time: 5 Mins   Cook Time: 5 Mins   Serves: 1

Ingredients:

- 1/2 Avocado no black spots
- 1/4 cup Unsweetened Almond Milk or unsweetened coconut milk
- 1/2 cup Baby Spinach
- 1 tablespoon Almond Butter
- 2 1/2 tablespoons Granulated Sweetener or stevia drops (pineapple stevia drops are good if you use coconut milk)
- 1/2 cup Ice Cubes
- 2 teaspoons Keto Collagen Protein Powder with MCT oil or keto vanilla protein powder
- 2 tablespoons Cocoa Nibs optional

Directions:

1. In a Ninja blender, add all the ingredients.
2. Blend until smooth and adjust with more ice cubes for a thicker smoothie. If too thick, add a splash of more almond milk and repeat blending between each addition.
3. Serve immediately.
4. Decorate with cocoa nibs and unsweetened coconut.

Nutritional Value (Amount per Serving):

Calories: 580; Fat: 47.04; Carb: 40.8; Protein: 11.11

Mango Spinach Smoothie

Prep Time: 5 Mins   Cook Time: 5 Mins   Serves: 1

Ingredients:

- 1 banana
- 1 handful fresh spinach
- 2 inches ginger
- 1/2 lemon juice only
- 10 mint leaves more if small leaves
- 1/4 cup coconut water divided
- 1/4 cup frozen mango

Directions:

1. Place all ingredients except coconut water in the blender. Pour in half of the coconut water, and blend until smooth and no whole pieces are left of the ginger or mango.
2. Add the rest of the coconut water and blend again, until smooth and creamy. Serve immediately!

Nutritional Value (Amount per Serving):

Calories: 479; Fat: 3.7; Carb: 113.24; Protein: 14.65

Ginger Smoothie With Spinach

Prep Time: 5 Mins   Cook Time: 5 Mins   Serves: 2

Ingredients:

- 1.5 cups unsweetened almond milk
- 1 tablespoon freshly grated ginger
- 1/2 stalk freshly grated turmeric, about 3 to 4 grams (optional)
- 2 frozen bananas, cut into chunks
- 1/2 cup chopped fresh pineapple (peeled)
- 2 generous handfuls baby spinach, about 2 loosely packed cups
- 2 tablespoons lemon juice, from about ½ of a lemon
- 1/2 cup crushed ice, optional

Directions:

1. Add all ingredients to a Ninja blender and blend until smooth.
2. Divide the smoothie between two glasses. Serve and enjoy!

Nutritional Value (Amount per Serving):

Calories: 407; Fat: 8.98; Carb: 79.49; Protein: 13.68

Fruity Green Ginger Smoothie

Prep Time: 5 Mins   Cook Time: 5 Mins   Serves: 2

Ingredients:

- 1 banana
- 1 apple peeled and cored
- 1 kiwi fruit peeled
- 1 teaspoon root ginger
- 1 handful spinach
- 200 ml cold water

Directions:

1. Put all the ingredients in a Ninja blender.
2. Blend for 1 minute.

Nutritional Value (Amount per Serving):

Calories: 315; Fat: 1.21; Carb: 80.85; Protein: 3.09

Green Smoothie

Prep Time: 5 Mins   Cook Time: 5 Mins   Serves: 2

Ingredients:

- 3 cups water
- 3 cups mango frozen
- 4 cups spinach
- 2 cups kale, coarsely chopped

Directions:

1. In a Ninja blender, add ingredients in the order listed above (don't change): water, mango, spinach and kale. Press "start" button and blend until smooth. I like to blend more for a super smooth smoothie.
2. Enjoy! What I love about this smoothie is that it doesn't separate much and tastes delicious even the next day.

Nutritional Value (Amount per Serving):

Calories: 170; Fat: 1.32; Carb: 40.65; Protein: 4.43

Avocado Spinach Smoothie

Prep Time: 6 Mins   Cook Time: 3 Mins   Serves: 2

Ingredients:

- 1 handful spinach
- 1 tbsp parsley, fresh
- 1/2 avocado
- 1 tsp cacao powder
- 1 tsp cinnamon
- 1/3 tsp sea salt
- 1 tbsp olive oil
- 1 tbsp walnuts (almonds are fine too)
- 1 tsp dark chocolate nibs
- 2 tsp coconut flakes
- 1/2 cup water (maybe a bit more)
- 1/2 tsp maple syrup (honey, if you are fine with that)
- 1/2 cup soy milk (milk would work too – just keep it gluten-free if necessary)
- 1 serving protein powder

Directions:

1. Throw everything into the Ninja blender and blend for 60 seconds.
2. Done.

Nutritional Value (Amount per Serving):

Calories: 278; Fat: 21.21; Carb: 17.41; Protein: 7.57

Detox Spinach Green Smoothie

Prep Time: 10 Mins   Cook Time: 5 Mins   Serves: 2

Ingredients:

- 2 bananas
- 1 apple
- 1 cup baby spinach
- 1 lemon
- 1 cup water, or as needed

Directions:

1. Peel bananas and an apple, cut into slices, and put into a Ninja blender.
2. Wash baby spinach and add to blender.
3. Squeeze the juice of 1 lemon (can be replaced with orange or lime) and add to the blender.

4. Add water as needed - about 1 cup.

5. Blend until smooth and serve.

Nutritional Value (Amount per Serving):

Calories: 402; Fat: 2.08; Carb: 103.05; Protein: 4.64

5-Minute Blueberry Spinach Smoothie

Prep Time: 5 Mins   Cook Time: 2 Mins   Serves: 1

Ingredients:

- 1 cup spinach
- 1 cup milk of choice, or to taste
- 1/2 cup plain Greek yogurt, or use coconut yogurt for a dairy-free option
- 1-1 1/2 cups frozen blueberries, if using fresh, add ice to the smoothie
- 1 very ripe banana, the riper the banana, the sweeter it will make your smoothie
- dash of cinnamon, optional

Directions:

1. Combine spinach, milk and yogurt in your blender. Blend until smooth and there are not bits of spinach left.
2. Add remaining ingredients and blend again.
3. Taste. Add extra milk or some water if a thinner consistency is desired.
4. Enjoy immediately.

Nutritional Value (Amount per Serving):

Calories: 363; Fat: 4.29; Carb: 68.43; Protein: 20

Pineapple Spinach Green Smoothie

Prep Time: 10 Mins   Cook Time: 5 Mins   Serves: 2

Ingredients:

- 1/2 pineapple
- 1 apple
- 1 orange, juice
- 1 cup young spinach leaves
- 1 passion fruit (optional)
- Water as needed

Directions:

1. Peel pineapple and cut into chunks. Slice and apple into quarters and remove the core. Cut orange in half and squeeze out the juice.

2. Place pineapple chunks, apple slices and orange juice in a Ninja blender. Add spinach leaves. Optionally, add the juice of a passion fruit. Add a splash of water and blend until smooth. If your smoothie is too thick, add more water as needed.

3. Pour smoothie into tall glasses and decorate with chia seeds and buckwheat cereals to taste. You can also skip this part and enjoy the smoothie as is.

Nutritional Value (Amount per Serving):

Calories: 189; Fat: 0.52; Carb: 47.39; Protein: 2.19

5-Minute Glowing Green Smoothie

Prep Time: 5 Mins   Cook Time: 5 Mins   Serves: 2

Ingredients:

- 1 banana, frozen, broken into chunks
- 3 mandarin oranges, peeled, (or 1 navel orange, peeled)
- 2 cups baby spinach, about 2 big handfuls
- 1 1/2 cups unsweetened non-dairy milk
- 1 tablespoon ground flax seeds
- 1 tablespoon chia seeds
- 1/2 teaspoon pure vanilla extract
- 1 cup ice, optional
- 2 scoops vanilla protein powder, optional

Directions:

1. Add all the ingredients to a Ninja blender. Blend until well combined. For a thinner consistency add additional milk.

Nutritional Value (Amount per Serving):

Calories: 1997; Fat: 176.64; Carb: 84.4; Protein: 31.97

Chapter 3: Smoothie Bowls

Tart Cherry Coconut Recovery Smoothie Bowl

Prep Time: 5 Mins   Cook Time: 5 Mins   Serves: 1

Ingredients:

- 1 scoop Iron-Tek Hydro Recovery
- 1 scoop, 18g vanilla whey protein powder (*see note)
- 1 cup frozen tart cherries
- 3/4 cup light coconut milk
- 1/8 teaspoon xanthan gum, optional for thickness

Directions:

1. Combine all ingredients for the smoothie in a Ninja blender. Blend until smooth.
2. Pour smoothie into a bowl and add desired toppings.

Nutritional Value (Amount per Serving):

Calories: 532; Fat: 43.68; Carb: 37.02; Protein: 7.24

Avocado Pineapple Smoothie Bowl

Prep Time: 10 Mins   Cook Time: 5 Mins   Serves: 2

Ingredients:

- 1 frozen banana
- 1 cup baby spinach
- 1/2 avocado
- 1 kiwi
- 1/2 cup frozen pineapple
- 1/2 tablespoon xanthan gum
- 3-4 leaves mint
- 1 cup unsweetened almond coconut milk
- 1 cup ice

Directions:

1. Combine all ingredients in a Ninja blender and blend until smooth.
2. Pour smoothie into bowls and garnish with desired toppings.

Nutritional Value (Amount per Serving):

Calories: 654; Fat: 40.64; Carb: 76.79; Protein: 8.45

Easy Tropical Spirulina Smoothie

Prep Time: 10 Mins   Cook Time: 5 Mins   Serves: 2

Ingredients:

- 1 cup baby greens, spinach, kale, arugula, etc.
- 3/4 cup frozen mango chunks, or pineapple
- 1/2 cup frozen banana
- 1/2 cup cucumber or frozen zucchini
- 1/4 cup frozen avocado chunks
- 1 kiwi
- 1 tablespoon ground flax seed
- 1/2 - 1 teaspoon spirulina powder
- 1 cup unsweetened almond milk or water, *see note
- 1 scoop protein powder/collagen of choice, optional

Directions:

1. Combine all ingredients in a Ninja blender and blend until smooth and creamy.
2. Pour into glasses or a bowl, and enjoy as is or with your favorite smoothie bowl toppings.

Nutritional Value (Amount per Serving):

Calories: 418; Fat: 10.19; Carb: 66.99; Protein: 20.66

Pumpkin Pie Smoothie Bowl

Prep Time: 5 Mins   Cook Time: 5 Mins   Serves: 1-2

Ingredients:

- 2 frozen ripe bananas, peeled prior to freezing
- 1/2 cup pumpkin puree, not pie filling
- 1–2 medjool dates, pitted
- 2 tbsp almond butter
- 1/2 tsp vanilla extract
- 1/2 tsp cinnamon
- 1/8 tsp nutmeg, optional
- 1/8 tsp allspice, optional
- 1/4 cup oat milk, or any plant-based milk

Directions:

1. Add all ingredients to a Ninja blender.
2. Blend ingredients until smooth and creamy.
3. Transfer smoothie to bowl(s). Add your favorite toppings. Enjoy!

Nutritional Value (Amount per Serving):

Calories: 386; Fat: 10.37; Carb: 73.01; Protein: 6.89

Mango Turmeric Smoothie Bowl

Prep Time: 5 Mins   Cook Time: 5 Mins   Serves: 1

Ingredients:

- 1/2 cup fresh mango
- 1 banana
- 1/2 cup probiotic yogurt
- 1/2 cup fresh orange juice
- 1 teaspoon turmeric powder
- 1 teaspoon vanilla extract

Directions:

1. Place mango, banana, yogurt, and orange juice in a Ninja blender. Mix well until you get a smooth mixture. Add vanilla and turmeric and mix again. Add a tablespoon or more water if the mixture is too thick.
2. Pour the mixture into the bowl. Decorate with toppings.
3. Serve immediately.

Nutritional Value (Amount per Serving):

Calories: 553; Fat: 6.35; Carb: 123.26; Protein: 9.96

Strawberry Ginger Smoothie Bowl

Prep Time: 5 Mins   Cook Time: 5 Mins   Serves: 1

Ingredients:

- 1 ripe banana
- 1 cup strawberries
- 1 teaspoon fresh ginger minced
- 1/2 teaspoon Ceylon cinnamon
- 1/2 teaspoon vanilla extract
- 1/2 cup almond milk unsweetened

Directions:

1. Peel the banana. Place it on baking paper on the plastic plate. Wash strawberries and dry them with paper towels. Slice them and place them on a plastic base with banana. Freeze for at least 4 hours.
2. Combine frozen banana, frozen strawberries, and almond milk in a Ninja blender. Puree until completely smooth - the mixture should be thick. Add

grated ginger, cinnamon, and vanilla. Blend the mixture.

3. Transfer mixture to a bowl and add toppings. Enjoy!

Nutritional Value (Amount per Serving):

Calories: 251; Fat: 7.8; Carb: 45.81; Protein: 2.85

Pina Colada Smoothie Bowl

Prep Time: 5 Mins   Cook Time: 5 Mins   Serves: 1

Ingredients:

- 1 banana - ripe
- 1 cup pineapple chunk – frozen
- 1/2 cup coconut milk ((full fat from a can))
- Sliced banana
- Toasted coconut chip

Directions:

1. First, toast a hand full of coconut chips in a skillet over medium heat until the edges are golden brown and the smell is toasty.
2. Put 1 banana, 1 cup pineapple and 1/2 cup of coconut milk in the blender and blend until smooth.
3. Pour smoothie into a bowl, garnish with slices of fresh or frozen banana and toasted coconut chips.
4. Serve immediately.

Nutritional Value (Amount per Serving):

Calories: 1117; Fat: 44.82; Carb: 188.61; Protein: 10.27

Easy Mango Smoothie Bowl

Prep Time: 10 Mins   Cook Time: 5 Mins   Serves: 2

Ingredients:

- 2 large mangoes (peeled, chopped & frozen)
- 1 cup coconut milk
- 1 cup almond milk
- 2 teaspoons honey
- 1 frozen banana

Directions:

1. Place the frozen mango, frozen banana, both milks and the honey in your blender and blend until smooth.
2. Divide the smoothie between two bowls. Top with toppings of your choice.

Nutritional Value (Amount per Serving):

Calories: 629; Fat: 31.64; Carb: 92.57; Protein: 6.82

Strawberry Acai Smoothie Bowl

Prep Time: 5 Mins   Cook Time: 5 Mins   Serves: 2

Ingredients:

- 1 Sambazon Açaí Performance Protein Superfruit Pack ((strawberry flavor))
- 1/2 cup frozen strawberries
- 1 banana
- 1/2 cup plain greek yogurt

Directions:

1. Mix all ingredients together in a Ninja blender.
2. Blend until completely smooth.
3. Add toppings and enjoy!

Nutritional Value (Amount per Serving):

Calories: 667; Fat: 1.41; Carb: 163.6; Protein: 8.07

Matcha Smoothie

Prep Time: 2 Mins   Cook Time: 5 Mins   Serves: 1

Ingredients:

- 1/4 cup almond milk (plus more as needed)
- 1 banana, peeled, sliced, and frozen
- 1 teaspoon matcha powder
- 1 cup fresh baby spinach, packed
- 1-2 pitted Medjool dates (see note)
- 1 tablespoon chia seeds
- 3 cubes ice
- 3 strawberries, sliced
- a few blueberries
- pinch of shredded coconut

Directions:

1. Pour the almond milk into the blender.
2. Top with banana, matcha powder, spinach, dates, and chia seeds.
3. Place the base on and blend.
4.
5. For a thick smoothie bowl add just enough liquid to turn the blender blade

and be patient. For a thinner, drinkable smoothie, add more liquid.
6. Blend until all green spinach bits are gone.
7. Transfer to a glass or bowl. Top with fruit and coconut if desired and enjoy right away!

Nutritional Value (Amount per Serving):

Calories: 907; Fat: 22.51; Carb: 177.23; Protein: 17.89

Creamy Dragon Fruit Smoothie Bowl

Prep Time: 5 Mins   Cook Time: 5 Mins   Serves: 2

Ingredients:

- 2 packets frozen dragon fruit (unsweetened)
- 1/2 cup frozen raspberries (or other fruit of choice)
- 2 medium ripe bananas previously peeled, sliced, and frozen
- 3 Tbsp Vegan Vanilla Protein Powder
- 1/4 – 1/2 cup dairy-free milk

Directions:

1. To a Ninja blender, add frozen dragon fruit, frozen raspberries, banana, protein powder, and dairy-free milk (starting with lower end of range). Blend until creamy and smooth. The trick to a thick smoothie bowl is being patient and blending slowly, adding only as much liquid as necessary.
2. Taste and adjust flavor as needed, adding more banana for sweetness, dairy-free milk for creaminess, or berries for more intense berry flavor.
3. Divide between serving bowls and enjoy as is or top with fruit, granola, hemp seeds, and coconut flakes (optional).
4. Best when fresh. Store leftovers in the refrigerator for up to 24 hours. Freeze for longer-term storage. Or freeze in ice cube mold to use in future smoothies.

Nutritional Value (Amount per Serving):

Calories: 321; Fat: 0.82; Carb: 70.45; Protein: 11.58

My Go-To Smoothie Bowl (5 minutes!)

Prep Time: 5 Mins   Cook Time: 5 Mins   Serves: 1

Ingredients:

- 1 heaping cup organic frozen mixed berries
- 1 small ripe banana (sliced and frozen)
- 2-3 Tbsp light coconut or almond milk (plus more as needed)

- 1 scoop plain or vanilla protein powder of choice* (optional)

Directions:

1. Add frozen berries and banana to a Ninja blender and blend on low until small bits remain – see photo.
2. Add a bit of coconut or almond milk and protein powder (optional), and blend on low again, until the mixture reaches a soft serve consistency (see photo).
3. Pour into 1-2 serving bowls and top with desired toppings (optional). I prefer chia seeds, hemp seeds, and coconut, but strawberries, granola, and a nut or seed butter would be great here, too!
4. Best when fresh, though leftovers keep in the freezer for 1-2 weeks. Let thaw before enjoying.

Nutritional Value (Amount per Serving):

Calories: 952; Fat: 25.56; Carb: 134.12; Protein: 48.46

Vegan Chocolate Smoothie Bowl Recipe

Prep Time: 2 Mins   Cook Time: 3 Mins   Serves: 1

Ingredients:

- 1 banana
- 1/2 cup spinach
- 2 dates pitted
- 1 tablespoon protein powder
- 1.5 tablespoon cacao powder
- 1 cup almond milk
- 1 tablespoon peanut butter
- 1 16 teaspoon salt
- 1 tablespoon oat flour optional

Directions:

1. Add the milk to the blender.
2. Add all the remaining ingredients.
3. Blend till smooth and enjoy.
4. The smoothie is best consumed immediately, but in case you have leftovers you can freeze them in ice cube tray or freezer safe container for up to a month.

Nutritional Value (Amount per Serving):

Calories: 627; Fat: 10.29; Carb: 132.3; Protein: 13.31

How To Make A Smoothie Bowl

Prep Time: 10 Mins   Cook Time: 5 Mins   Serves: 1

Ingredients:

- Small frozen banana, sliced OR 1 cup cauliflower
- 1 cup frozen fruit of choice - we used mixed berries but strawberries, pineapple, mangos, etc. all work great!
- 1/4 cup liquid of choice - we used almond milk but any milk or juice will work
- Optional scoop of protein powder
- Optional spoonful of nut butter
- Toppings of your choice - granola, nuts and seeds, sliced fruit, freeze dried fruit, nut butter, coconut flakes, etc. etc.

Directions:

1. Add the frozen banana (or cauliflower) and fruit to the blender and blend on low. The goal of this step is to chop the frozen fruit into small bits - which will make blending later a breeze. The fruit will bounce all around the blender as it gets chopped into small pieces.
2. Add milk and blend until smooth. Blend until the little fruit bits turn into a smooth mixture. You may need to scrape down the sides a few times to "unstick" the blender.
3. Once smooth, add in optional protein powder, nut butter, and other superfoods. Blend again, until smooth.
4. Pour into a bowl, cover with toppings, and ENJOY!

Nutritional Value (Amount per Serving):

Calories: 778; Fat: 26.7; Carb: 117.3; Protein: 28.26

Acai Smoothie Bowl

Prep Time: 10 Mins   Cook Time: 5 Mins   Serves: 1

Ingredients:

- 1 frozen banana, sliced
- 1/2-3/4 cup frozen berries
- 1 frozen unsweetened acai packet, broken into a few pieces
- 1/4-1/2 cup almond milk

Directions:

1. Add the banana, berries and frozen acai puree to your blender. Let it sit in the blender for 2-3 minutes to soften slightly. Turn on the blender and let it chop up the fruit into small pieces.

2. Add in the milk and blend until smooth.

Nutritional Value (Amount per Serving):

Calories:576; Fat: 25.09; Carb: 82.23; Protein: 23.86

Banana Smoothie Bowl

Prep Time: 10 Mins   Cook Time: 5 Mins   Serves: 1

Ingredients:

- 2 frozen bananas, peeled and sliced
- 1/4 cup milk - almond, soy, etc.
- 1-2 tablespoons nut butter
- Pinch cinnamon, optional

Directions:

1. Add the bananas to the blender. Let it sit in the blender for 2-3 minutes. Turn on the blender and let it chop up the fruit into small pieces.
2. Add in the milk and blend until smooth.

Nutritional Value (Amount per Serving):

Calories: 394; Fat: 14.88; Carb: 66.14; Protein: 8.08

Dragon Fruit Smoothie Bowl

Prep Time: 10 Mins   Cook Time: 5 Mins   Serves: 1

Ingredients:

- 1 frozen banana, sliced
- 1 dragon fruit puree packet
- 1/4 cup frozen pineapple
- 1/4 cup frozen mango
- 1/4-1/2 cup orange juice or milk
- 1-2 tablespoons peanut butter, optional

Directions:

1. Add your fruit to the blender. Let it sit in the blender for 2-3 minutes. Turn on the blender and let it chop up the fruit into small pieces.
2. Add in the milk and blend until smooth.

Nutritional Value (Amount per Serving):

Calories: 619; Fat: 5.16; Carb: 149.65; Protein: 5.25

Chapter 4: Dairy Free Smoothies

Dairy Free Cranberry Smoothie

Prep Time: 5 Mins   Cook Time: 5 Mins   Serves: 1

Ingredients:

- 3/4 cup (75 grams) frozen cranberries
- 1 large apple, cored and chopped into chunks
- 1 small handful (about 2 tablespoons) raw pecans or walnuts, or 2 tablespoons of nut butter
- 1 tablespoon maple syrup , or agave
- 1 cup non-dairy milk
- 1/4 teaspoon ground cinnamon

Directions:

1. Add all the ingredients to a Ninja blender.
2. Blend until smooth.

Nutritional Value (Amount per Serving):

Calories: 2646; Fat: 231.13; Carb: 156.52; Protein: 0.76

Dairy Free Vegan Mango Smoothie

Prep Time: 5 Mins   Cook Time: 5 Mins   Serves: 2

Ingredients:

- 1 small Banana - fresh, ripe, cut in pieces
- 1 cup dairy-free yogurt
- 2 cups Frozen Mango
- 1 cup Unsweetened Vanilla Almond Milk

Directions:

1. In a Ninja blender, add banana pieces, yogurt, frozen mango, and almond milk.
2. Blend until thick and smooth, adding more almond milk if it's difficult to blend or too thick for you.
3. Serve immediately.

Nutritional Value (Amount per Serving):

Calories: 264; Fat: 6.02; Carb: 49.87; Protein: 6.66

Dairy Free Papaya Smoothie

Prep Time: 10 Mins   Cook Time: 10 Mins   Serves: 1

Ingredients:

- 1 cup Papaya (about 1/2 medium papaya sliced and peeled)
- 1 cup Fresh pineapple chunks
- 2 ripe Bananas sliced
- 1/4 cup Coconut water
- 2 tbsp Agave
- 1/4 tsp Ground ginger

Directions:

1. Place all the ingredients into a Ninja blender and blend until everything is smooth.
2. Serve and enjoy.

Nutritional Value (Amount per Serving):

Calories: 1034; Fat: 4.65; Carb: 263.03; Protein: 10.47

Apple Pie Smoothie

Prep Time: 5 Mins   Cook Time: 5 Mins   Serves: 2

Ingredients:

- 1 cup unsweetened, plain non-dairy milk plus more if needed
- 2 medium apples cored and rough chopped
- 2 tablespoons raw walnuts chopped
- 1 tablespoon flax meal ground flax seeds
- 1 teaspoon pure vanilla extract
- 1 teaspoon ground cinnamon or to taste
- 1/2 teaspoon ground nutmeg or to taste
- 2-3 ice cubes

Directions:

1. Place all ingredients in a Ninja blender and puree until smooth.
2. Pour into a glass and savor the flavors of fall!

Nutritional Value (Amount per Serving):

Calories: 1253; Fat: 124.39; Carb: 36.26; Protein: 4.8

Apple Banana Smoothie

Prep Time: 5 Mins   Cook Time: 5 Mins   Serves: 1-2

Ingredients:

- 1 sweet apple, core and seeds removed

- 1 ripe banana (frozen banana is ideal, but fresh banana works too)
- 3/4 cup non-dairy milk
- 2 tablespoons peanut butter (smooth or crunchy)
- 1/4 teaspoon vanilla extract
- pinch of cinnamon
- 1/2 cup of ice (you can leave out this ice if using frozen banana)

Directions:

1. Add all of your ingredients to a Ninja blender. Blend until smooth. Add more liquid to thin out the smoothie if needed.
2. Divide between 1 or 2 glasses and enjoy.

Nutritional Value (Amount per Serving):

Calories: 945; Fat: 89.19; Carb: 38.46; Protein: 3.11

Easy Oat Milk Smoothie

Prep Time: 5 Mins   Cook Time: 5 Mins   Serves: 1

Ingredients:

- 1 frozen banana, cut into chunks
- 4 ice cubes
- 1/2 tsp cinnamon
- 1 tablespoon pure maple syrup
- 1 tablespoon natural peanut butter or almond butter (optional)
- 1/2 cup unsweetened oat milk
- 1/4 cup vanilla plant-based protein powder of choice or unflavoured collagen peptides (optional)

Directions:

1. Add the frozen banana, ice, cinnamon, maple syrup, and nut butter (if using) to the blender.
2. Pour in the oat milk.
3. Add in the protein powder (if using).
4. Blend until smooth, pour into a glass, and enjoy!

Nutritional Value (Amount per Serving):

Calories: 669; Fat: 24.99; Carb: 87.2; Protein: 37.83

Healthy Vegan Oreo Smoothie

Prep Time: 5 Mins   Cook Time: 5 Mins   Serves: 1

Ingredients:

- 1 frozen banana [for less banana flavor, use 1/2 frozen banana and 1 cup of ice]
- 3/4 cup vegan milk
- 2-4 Oreos
- 1 tsp Vanilla extract

Directions:

1. In a Ninja blender, add all ingredients and blend until smooth and creamy.
2. Taste and adjust the flavor according to your preference.
3. Serve in a tall glass and garnish with vegan whipped cream and an Oreo if you aren't going too "healthy" and want to add something fun. Otherwise, enjoy the vegan milkshake as-is!

Nutritional Value (Amount per Serving):

Calories: 356; Fat: 8.78; Carb: 58.33; Protein: 9.42

Chocolate Avocado Smoothie

Prep Time: 10 Mins   Cook Time: 5 Mins   Serves: 2

Ingredients:

- 1 cup Almond Milk
- 1/2 large Avocado - ripe, with no black spots
- 4-6 Soft Pitted Dates - or 2 tablespoons of maple syrup or coconut sugar
- 2 1/2 tablespoons Unsweetened Cocoa Powder
- 1 cup Ice Cubes
- 1 teaspoon Vanilla Extract
- 1 small Banana - sliced

Directions:

1. Before you start, make sure your avocado has no black spot. If so, it means it is too ripe and it will add a bitter taste to your smoothie. You need a ripe avocado with smooth green flesh.
2. In a Ninja blender, add all the ingredients together, starting with 4 dates. Adjust the amount in the next step if not sweet enough.
3. Blend until frothy and thick. Taste and adjust the number of dates, adding up to 2 Medjool dates to boost the sweetness.
4. Serve immediately with unsweetened coconut whipped cream, chocolate chips, or melted chocolate.

Nutritional Value (Amount per Serving):

Calories: 400; Fat: 11.08; Carb: 75.25; Protein: 4.65

White Chocolate Strawberry Cake Smoothie

Prep Time: 10 Mins   Cook Time: 10 Mins   Serves: 2

Ingredients:

- 1 1/4 cups unsweetened cashew milk
- 2-3 tablespoons (40-60g) pure maple syrup
- 3 tablespoons RAW cashew butter (not roasted and with no added oil, it will ruin the flavor)
- 1 teaspoon vanilla powder
- 1/8 teaspoon fine sea salt
- 3 tablespoons (40g) melted cocoa butter
- 2 cups (280g) or One 10 oz bag FROZEN strawberries
- Vegan Sprinkles
- Coconut cream for topping (optional)

Directions:

1. Add all of the ingredients, except the frozen strawberries to a Ninja blender and process until very smooth.
2. Add the strawberries and process just until combined and thick.
3. Serve immediately.

Nutritional Value (Amount per Serving):

Calories: 462; Fat: 33.19; Carb: 32.96; Protein: 9.99

Banana Chocolate Pistachio Smoothie

Prep Time: 10 Mins   Cook Time: 10 Mins   Serves: 1

Ingredients:

- 1 cup spinach or kale optional
- 1 large banana, frozen and cut into chunks
- 1 Tablespoon cocoa powder
- 2 Tablespoons pistachios
- 1 cup Silk Unsweetened Vanilla Almondmilk
- 1/2 cup ice cubes, or more or less based on desired consistency
- additional chopped pistachios or dairy free chocolate chips optional

Directions:

1. Add ingredients to the blender in the order listed (except the optional chopped pistachios and dairy free chocolate chips) and blend to desired consistency.
2. Pour into a glass and serve, topping with chopped pistachios and dairy free chocolate chips if desired.

Nutritional Value (Amount per Serving):

Calories: 846; Fat: 31.28; Carb: 135.63; Protein: 20.64

Maple Cinnamon Blueberry Smoothie

Prep Time: 5 Mins   Cook Time: 5 Mins   Serves: 2

Ingredients:

- 1 cup baby spinach leaves
- 1 cup frozen blueberries
- 5.3 oz Silk Blueberry Dairy-Free Yogurt Alternative or Blueberry Greek yogurt (can use plain but you may need to add additional syrup or other sweetener.)
- 1 teaspoon pure maple syrup
- 1 teaspoon cinnamon
- 1 cup Silk Unsweetened Vanilla Almondmilk or your milk of choice
- 4 small ice cubes or more for a thicker smoothie

Directions:

1. Add all of the ingredients except the ice to your blender and blend until smooth.
2. Add ice and blend to achieve desired consistency.

Nutritional Value (Amount per Serving):

Calories: 374; Fat: 16.3; Carb: 57; Protein: 3.74

Vegan Chocolate Coffee Smoothie

Prep Time: 5 Mins   Cook Time: 5 Mins   Serves: 2

Ingredients:

- 2 cups Vanilla Bean Coconut Ice Cream
- 1-2 Tbsp unsweetened cocoa or cacao powder
- 1/2 - 3/4 cup brewed coffee (chilled // medium to bold roast is best)
- 2-4 Tbsp unsweetened almond or coconut milk (optional)
- Vegan Magic Shell and/or Coconut Whipped Cream (optional // for topping)

Directions:

1. Add ice cream, cocoa powder (starting with lesser amount), and coffee (starting with lesser amount) to a Ninja blender and blend until creamy and smooth. Add more coffee or almond milk (optional) if it has trouble blending.

2. Taste and adjust ingredients as needed, adding more cocoa powder for more chocolate flavor, coffee for more coffee flavor, or almond milk for creaminess (optional).
3. Divide between 2 serving glasses and top with Coconut Whipped Cream (optional) or Vegan Magic Shell (optional).

Nutritional Value (Amount per Serving):

Calories: 350; Fat: 23.01; Carb: 33.14; Protein: 5.57

Dairy-free Vanilla Date Smoothie

Prep Time: 5 Mins   Cook Time: 5 Mins   Serves: 1

Ingredients:

- 1 cup unsweetened almond milk (use your favorite non-dairy milk)
- 1 medium frozen banana
- 4-5 ice cubes (or another frozen banana)
- 2-3 medjool dates, pitted (soft and fresh is best)
- 1 teaspoon vanilla extract

Directions:

1. Combine ingredients into the Ninja blender cup and blend until smooth, about 1-2 minutes, depending on your blender.
2. Add a splash or two of extra almond milk as needed, especially if adding protein powder.

Nutritional Value (Amount per Serving):

Calories: 876; Fat: 5.23; Carb: 216.26; Protein: 9.67

Vegan Pumpkin Smoothie

Prep Time: 5 Mins   Cook Time: 5 Mins   Serves: 2

Ingredients:

- 2 cups non-dairy vanilla ice cream
- 1/2 cup canned pumpkin puree
- 1/2 cup non-dairy milk
- 1/2 teaspoon pumpkin pie spice
- Vegan Whipped Cream

Directions:

1. In a Ninja blender, blend together non-dairy ice cream, pumpkin puree, non-dairy milk and pumpkin pie spice.
2. Pour into glasses and garnish with non-dairy whipped cream. I used

almond whipped cream from the store, but you could make your own Vegan Whipped Cream if you want.

Nutritional Value (Amount per Serving):

Calories: 845; Fat: 71.79; Carb: 42.8; Protein: 10.16

Dairy-free Cookie Dough Smoothie

Prep Time: 5 Mins   Cook Time: 5 Mins   Serves: 2

Ingredients:

- 3 cups Dairy-free cookie dough ice cream (I love So Delicious Dairy-Free)
- 1 cup Almond Milk (See Notes!)
- 1 teaspoon vanilla extract
- Pinch of sea salt

Directions:

1. Add the cookie dough ice cream, milk, vanilla, and salt, to the blender and blend until smooth, about 1-2 minutes.
2. Once milkshake consistency is met, pour milkshake into tall glass(es), and top each milkshake with coconut whipped cream, chopped chocolate or cookies, and coconut flakes, if desired.
3. Add a straw and sip away and enjoy!

Nutritional Value (Amount per Serving):

Calories: 494; Fat: 26.65; Carb: 55.54; Protein: 7.03

Smoothie King Peanut Power Plus Chocolate Smoothie

Prep Time: 5 Mins   Cook Time: 5 Mins   Serves: 2

Ingredients:

- 1 medium banana
- 1 tablespoon Hershey's Cocoa (unsweetened)
- 2 tablespoons Creamy Peanut Butter
- 1 cup almond milk (unsweetened, vanilla)
- 1 scoop of protein (chocolate flavored)
- 1/4 cup nonfat yogurt (plain)
- 3 dates

Directions:

1. Add all ingredients (plus one cup of ice) into a Ninja blender. Blend until

smooth.

2. Pour smoothie into a glass and enjoy!

Nutritional Value (Amount per Serving):

Calories: 446; Fat: 11.79; Carb: 83.96; Protein: 9.59

Homemade Vanilla Almond Milk Smoothie

Prep Time: 6hrs   Cook Time: 10 Mins   Serves: 1-2

Ingredients:

- 1 cup raw almonds
- 4 cups filtered water (plus more for soaking overnight)
- 1 teaspoon vanilla extract
- 1 tablespoon honey
- Pinch of sea salt

Directions:

1. Add almonds to a bowl and cover with enough water to submerge. Soak 6-8 hours or overnight. This helps them soften enough so that they can blend properly.
2. In the morning, drain almonds from their soaking water and rinse them in a colander.
3. Add soaked almonds and 4 cups of fresh filtered water to the blender. Add in vanilla, honey and salt.
4. Blend for 1 minute, adding 30 seconds more if you feel it necessary to blend.
5. Place your nut milk bag over a large bowl or pitcher. Pour the almond milk into the bag and strain the liquid into the bowl, using your hands to wring out all of the milk.
6. Pour the almond milk from the bowl into glass jars. Almond milk will keep in the fridge for up to a week, if not longer. If it separates, simply shake the jars.

Nutritional Value (Amount per Serving):

Calories: 41; Fat: 0.3; Carb: 9.15; Protein: 0.16

Raspberry Coconut Cloud Smoothie

Prep Time: 10 Mins   Cook Time: 5 Mins   Serves: 1

Ingredients:

- 3/4 Cup Frozen Raspberries

- 1 Frozen Banana
- 1/3 Cup + 2 Tablespoons Canned Coconut Cream divided
- 1 Cup Unsweetened Vanilla Almond Milk plus more to thin, if needed
- 2 Tablespoons Rolled Oats
- 1/4 Teaspoon Cinnamon
- 1/8 Teaspoon Nutmeg
- 1/4 Teaspoon Ground Ginger
- 1/2 Teaspoon Vanilla Extract

Directions:

1. Add all of the smoothie ingredients (minus the 2 tablespoons of coconut cream) to the blender and blend until smooth. You may need to stop the blender and add more almond milk as desired, to thin out the smoothie.
2. Next, grab your glass and add the two tablespoons of coconut cream to the bottom. Use a spoon to spread the coconut cream up the sides of the glass.
3. Pour the smoothie in the glass, and top with additional coconut cream and/or chopped fresh raspberries, if desired.
4. Serve immediately, and enjoy!

Nutritional Value (Amount per Serving):

Calories: 961; Fat: 33.55; Carb: 174.26; Protein: 11.72

Butternut Squash Smoothie

Prep Time: 10 Mins   Cook Time: 10 Mins   Serves: 1

Ingredients:

- 1 cup frozen cubed roasted butternut squash
- 1 cup unsweetened plain almond milk, or milk of choice
- 3/4 cup frozen strawberries
- 1/2 cup frozen riced cauliflower
- 1 tablespoon ground flaxseed
- 1 tablespoon chia seeds
- 1 tablespoon almond butter
- 1-2 pitted medjool dates, adjust for desired sweetness
- 1 slice fresh ginger, substitute 1/4 teaspoon ground ginger spice
- 1/2 teaspoon vanilla extract
- 1/4 teaspoon cinnamon
- 1/8 teaspoon cardamom
- 1 scoop collagen or protein powder of choice, optional

Directions:

1. Combine all ingredients in the blender and blend until smooth.
2. Pour into a glass and enjoy!

Nutritional Value (Amount per Serving):

Calories: 824; Fat: 28.68; Carb: 107.11; Protein: 46.83

Greek Yogurt Smoothie

Prep Time: 5 Mins   Cook Time: 5 Mins   Serves: 1

Ingredients:

- 1 cup frozen mixed berries, (I used strawberries, blueberries, raspberries, and blackberries)
- 1/2 cup vanilla Greek yogurt
- 2 large handfuls of spinach
- 1/2 cup unsweetened vanilla almond milk
- 2 teaspoons Chia seeds, optional, but they're such a great superfood
- 1 scoop collagen powder or protein powder, optional

Directions:

1. Place all ingredients into blender and blend until smooth. You can add more ice or almond milk to achieve a desired consistency, but I find that the listed amounts of ingredients produce a really great smoothie texture.

Nutritional Value (Amount per Serving):

Calories: 449; Fat: 14.33; Carb: 54.44; Protein: 29.45

Chapter 5: Protein Shakes

Perfect Protein-packed Breakfast Shake

Prep Time: 5 Mins   Cook Time: 5 Mins   Serves: 1

Ingredients:

- 200 ml milk
- 100 ml brewed coffee
- 1 Latte or Chocolate flavoured Impact Whey Protein
- 1 tbsp maple syrup
- 100 g banana
- 1 tsp cocoa powder

Directions:

1. Add all ingredients to the blender.
2. Add ice cubes or vanilla ice for extra texture/taste.

Nutritional Value (Amount per Serving):

Calories: 517; Fat: 6.15; Carb: 115.37; Protein: 11.14

Wake-Up Bittersweet Matcha Whey Protein Shake

Prep Time: 5 Mins   Cook Time: 5 Mins   Serves: 1

Ingredients:

- 1 Scoop (25g) Matcha Whey Protein
- 2 medium-sized peaches
- 1/2 thumb root ginger (grated)
- 75ml milk (of choice)

Directions:

1. Chop the peaches and place into blender, along with matcha whey, ginger and milk, and blend until smooth.

Nutritional Value (Amount per Serving):

Calories: 269; Fat: 2.67; Carb: 43.09; Protein: 22.15

Breakfast Protein Shake

Prep Time: 5 Mins   Cook Time: 5 Mins   Serves: 1-2

Ingredients:

- 200ml almond milk or dairy-free milk of choice
- 1 tbsp. rolled oats
- 2 pitted dates

- 1 tbsp. hazelnuts
- 1 scoop Vegan Blend or Impact Whey Protein
- 1 tsp. Chia Seeds
- Pinch sea salt

Directions:

1. Simply add all ingredients to the blender and process until smooth.
2. Pour into a glass or shaker and top with a couple of extra dates and nuts if you're feeling fancy.

Nutritional Value (Amount per Serving):

Calories: 208; Fat: 8.15; Carb: 25.01; Protein: 11.89

Superfood Green Protein Shake

Prep Time: 5 Mins   Cook Time: 5 Mins   Serves: 1

Ingredients:

- 1 scoop Superfood Protein Blend
- 200ml coconut water
- 1 apple
- 2 carrots
- 1/2 cucumber
- 2 celery stalks
- 1/2 lemon (juice)
- Handful ice cubes

Directions:

1. Simply blend all ingredients together and serve.

Nutritional Value (Amount per Serving):

Calories: 8188; Fat: 93.12; Carb: 1582.64; Protein: 312.82

Meal Replacement Protein Shake

Prep Time: 5 Mins   Cook Time: 5 Mins   Serves: 1

Ingredients:

- 250ml milk (of choice)
- 250ml water
- 3 scoops Vanilla Raspberry Whole Fuel Blend
- 50g fresh raspberries

Directions:

1. Simply place all ingredients into a Ninja blender and process until creamy

and smooth.

Nutritional Value (Amount per Serving):

Calories:154; Fat: 5.31; Carb: 18.65; Protein: 8.92

Energizing Peach Protein Shake

Prep Time: 10 Mins   Cook Time: 5 Mins   Serves: 1

Ingredients:

- 200ml skimmed milk
- 400g tinned peaches
- 1 scoop Vanilla Impact Whey Protein
- 10g Beetroot Powder
- 5g Guarana Extract
- 5g Creatine Monohydrate
- 6-8 cubes ice

Directions:

1. Simply blend all ingredients together until smooth.
2. Drink 60-90 minutes before your workout.

Nutritional Value (Amount per Serving):

Calories: 971; Fat: 37.07; Carb: 119.88; Protein: 44.76

Post-workout Banana Vanilla Protein Shake

Prep Time: 10 Mins   Cook Time: 5 Mins   Serves: 1-2

Ingredients:

- 1 scoop (35g) Maltodextrin
- 5g L-Leucine
- 1g HMB
- 1-2 scoops Vanilla Impact Whey Isolate
- 1 ripe banana
- 200ml skimmed milk/water

Directions:

1. Simply place all ingredients in a Ninja blender and process until smooth. Consume within 1 hour after your workout for maximum benefits.

Nutritional Value (Amount per Serving):

Calories: 223; Fat: 11.52; Carb: 18.84; Protein: 12.2

Salted Caramel Protein Shake

Prep Time: 10 Mins   Cook Time: 5 Mins   Serves: 1

Ingredients:

- 1 scoop Salted Caramel Impact Whey Protein
- 1 scoop Instant Oats or rolled oats blended to a fine powder
- 1 small banana
- 1 tbsp. Almond Butter
- 250ml whole milk

Directions:

1. Simply blend all ingredients together until smooth and enjoy.

Nutritional Value (Amount per Serving):

Calories: 540; Fat: 17.84; Carb: 70.33; Protein: 30.57

Mint Chocolate Protein Shake

Prep Time: 5 Mins   Cook Time: 5 Mins   Serves: 1

Ingredients:

- 1 scoop Chocolate Mint Impact Whey Protein
- 1/2 tsp. peppermint extract
- 300ml almond milk
- 25g Cacao Nibs

Directions:

1. Simply blend all ingredients together and drink straight after your workout.

Nutritional Value (Amount per Serving):

Calories: 314; Fat: 14.52; Carb: 42.69; Protein: 4.03

Raspberry Protein Shake

Prep Time: 5 Mins   Cook Time: 5 Mins   Serves: 1

Ingredients:

- 100g frozen raspberries
- 250ml skimmed milk
- 2 tbsp. quark or Greek yogurt
- 1/2 banana
- 1 scoop Raspberry Impact Whey Protein

Directions:

1. Simply add all ingredients to a Ninja blender and blend until smooth.

Nutritional Value (Amount per Serving):

Calories: 743; Fat: 22.17; Carb: 92.92; Protein: 48.87

Strawberry Mint Protein Shake

Prep Time: 10 Mins   Cook Time: 5 Mins   Serves: 1

Ingredients:

- 1 scoop Thewhey (Strawberry Milkshake Flavour)
- Handful fresh mint leaves
- 4 tbsp. Greek yoghurt
- 100ml milk
- Handful frozen berries

Directions:

1. Simply place all ingredients in a Ninja blender and blitz until smooth.
2. Add a little honey after a tough workout for glycogen replenishment.

Nutritional Value (Amount per Serving):

Calories: 125; Fat: 3.55; Carb: 15.23; Protein: 9.8

Honey Banana Protein Shake

Prep Time: 5 Mins   Cook Time: 3 Mins   Serves: 1

Ingredients:

- 1 frozen banana
- 25g Organic Whey Protein
- 1 tsp. honey
- 1 tsp. cinnamon
- 10g Bee Pollen

Directions:

1. Blend all ingredients together and serve.
2. For an extra boost, sprinkle some additional bee pollen or add a few raw cacao nibs on top.

Nutritional Value (Amount per Serving):

Calories: 464; Fat: 2.13; Carb: 103.49; Protein: 18.55

Strawberry Protein Shake

Prep Time: 5 Mins   Cook Time: 5 Mins   Serves: 1

Ingredients:

- 2 kiwi fruit (peeled)
- 1/2 pint apple juice or water
- 5 large strawberries
- 1 scoop Strawberry Impact Whey Protein
- 1/2 tbsp. Manuka Honey
- 1 cup ice cubes
- 1/2 lime (juice)

Directions:

1. Peel the kiwi fruit using a knife, then add all ingredients to a Ninja blender and process until smooth.

Nutritional Value (Amount per Serving):

Calories: 692; Fat: 17.68; Carb: 115.79; Protein: 22.73

Vanilla Creme Frappe

Prep Time: 5 Mins   Cook Time: 5 Mins   Serves: 1

Ingredients:

- 1 scoop Vanilla Creme Thewhey protein powder
- 1/2 tsp. ground ginger or ½ thumb fresh ginger (peeled)
- 1/2 tsp. cinnamon
- 250ml milk (of choice)
- 8 ice cubes
- Drizzle Sugar-Free Syrup
- Crumbled Baked Cookie (optional)

Directions:

1. First, blend whey protein, ground ginger/fresh ginger, cinnamon, milk and ice cubes, and process until slushy.
2. Drizzle syrup around the sides of the glass or shaker and pour the mixture into the glass.

Nutritional Value (Amount per Serving):

Calories: 387; Fat: 11.77; Carb: 38.34; Protein: 34.67

Post-workout Protein Shake

Prep Time: 5 Mins   Cook Time: 5 Mins   Serves: 1

Ingredients:

- 1 scoop Wellness Superfood Blend
- 250ml coconut milk
- 1/2 frozen banana
- 1 tsp. cinnamon
- 30g rolled oats

Directions:

1. Simply blend all ingredients together and serve.

Nutritional Value (Amount per Serving):

Calories: 930; Fat: 70.74; Carb: 80.45; Protein: 19.65

Pea Protein Sundae Shake

Prep Time: 5 Mins   Cook Time: 5 Mins   Serves: 1-2

Ingredients:

- 1 scoop Pea Protein
- 1 large banana
- 250ml dairy-free milk
- 4-6 drops Toffee FlavDrops
- ½ tsp. cinnamon
- Handful popcorn to garnish

Directions:

1. Simply blend all ingredients except popcorn, and process until smooth.
2. Top with extra cinnamon and the popcorn.

Nutritional Value (Amount per Serving):

Calories: 347; Fat: 7.43; Carb: 65.09; Protein: 8.24

Blueberry Banana Swirl Protein Shake

Prep Time: 5 Mins   Cook Time: 5 Mins   Serves: 1

Ingredients:

- 1 scoop Pea Protein
- 50g frozen blueberries
- 100ml dairy-free milk
- 100ml dairy-free yoghurt
- 1 small banana
- 2-4 drops Vanilla FlavDrops

Directions:

1. Blend together pea protein, blueberries and milk until smooth, then pour

into the glass halfway.

2. Then blend together the banana and yoghurt, then layer on top of the blueberry mixture.

3. Swirl the layers together using a spoon, top with a few extra blueberries.

Nutritional Value (Amount per Serving):

Calories: 231; Fat: 1.07; Carb: 44.15; Protein: 6.85

Delicious Post-workout Protein Shake

Prep Time: 5 Mins   Cook Time: 5 Mins   Serves: 1

Ingredients:

- 1 scoop (25g) Vegan Blend Chocolate Smooth flavour
- 250ml almond milk
- 50g blueberries
- 1 banana
- Handful of spinach or kale

Directions:

1. Simply blend all ingredients until smooth, and consume straight after a workout for maximum benefits.

Nutritional Value (Amount per Serving):

Calories: 608; Fat: 5.69; Carb: 143.73; Protein: 7.6

Strawberry BCAA Protein Shake

Prep Time: 5 Mins   Cook Time: 5 Mins   Serves: 1

Ingredients:

- 8 scoops Peach Tea BCAA
- 10 strawberries, plus extra to decorate
- 1 lime (juice)
- 75ml water
- 3 large handfuls ice

Directions:

1. Place all ingredients into a Ninja blender and process until slushy. You don't want to overdo it here - just blend enough before it liquefies too much.
2. Pour into shot glasses and decorate each glass with a fresh strawberry. Perfection!

Nutritional Value (Amount per Serving):

Calories: 327; Fat: 14.56; Carb: 49.64; Protein: 4.57

Chapter 6: Frozen Drinks

Blended Raspberry Martini

Prep Time: 5 Mins   Cook Time: 5 Mins   Serves: 1

Ingredients:

- 1 package raspberry crystal light
- 2 cups ginger ale
- 1/2 cup vodka
- 2 cups crushed ice
- Fresh raspberries for garnish

Directions:

1. In a Ninja blender, combine the crystal light, ginger ale, vodka, and ice.
2. Cover and blend until smooth. Pour into a martini glass and garnish with fresh raspberries.

Nutritional Value (Amount per Serving):

Calories: 835; Fat: 42.06; Carb: 106.68; Protein: 9.93

Refreshing Watermelon Cocktail

Prep Time: 10 Mins   Cook Time: 5 Mins   Serves: 1-2

Ingredients:

- 1 1/2 cups cubed watermelon
- 2 ounces vodka
- 1/2 teaspoon grenadine
- 1/2 cup crushed ice
- Watermelon wedge for garnish

Directions:

1. In a Ninja blender, combine the watermelon, vodka, grenadine, and ice.
2. Cover and blend until smooth.
3. Pour into a highball glass and garnish with a wedge of watermelon.

Nutritional Value (Amount per Serving):

Calories: 134; Fat: 6.25; Carb: 18.7; Protein: 2.12

Frozen Banana

Prep Time: 5 Mins   Cook Time: 5 Mins   Serves: 1

Ingredients:

- 1 banana, peeled and sliced

- 1 ounce banana liqueur
- 1 cup pineapple juice
- 2 ounces RumChata
- 1 cup crushed ice

Directions:

1. In a Ninja blender, combine the banana, banana liqueur, pineapple juice, RumChata, and ice.
2. Cover and blend until smooth.
3. Pour into a highball glass.

Nutritional Value (Amount per Serving):

Calories: 879; Fat: 19.29; Carb: 181.79; Protein: 10.22

Frozen Peaches and Cream

Prep Time: 5 Mins   Cook Time: 5 Mins   Serves: 1

Ingredients:

- 2 fresh peaches, pitted and sliced
- 1 ounce peach schnapps
- 2 ounces RumChata
- 1 cup milk or half-and half
- 1 scoop vanilla ice cream

Directions:

1. In a Ninja blender, combine all ingredients.
2. Cover and blend until smooth.
3. Serve in a highball glass.

Nutritional Value (Amount per Serving):

Calories: 584; Fat: 6.25; Carb: 133.12; Protein: 11.76

Frozen Hula Hoop

Prep Time: 5 Mins   Cook Time: 5 Mins   Serves: 2

Ingredients:

- 6 cups ice cubes
- 1/2 cup plus 1 tablespoon (4 1/2 ounces) white rum
- 1/2 cup plus 1 tablespoon fresh or canned pineapple juice
- 1/4 cup plus 2 tablespoons raspberry syrup (see Note)
- 1/4 cup plus 1/2 tablespoon (2 1/4 ounces) dry red wine (such as Shiraz)
- 1/4 cup plus 1/2 tablespoon fresh lemon juice

- 3 tablespoons (1 1/2 ounces) Aperol
- Pineapple fronds, edible orchids, and raspberries, for garnish

Directions:

1. Process ice cubes, rum, pineapple juice, raspberry syrup, wine, lemon juice, and Aperol in a Ninja blender until smooth, about 30 seconds.
2. Pour evenly into tulip glasses or snifters. If desired, garnish with pineapple fronds, orchids, and raspberries.

Nutritional Value (Amount per Serving):

Calories: 994; Fat: 50.93; Carb: 111.16; Protein: 14

Frozen Shirley Temple

Prep Time: 3 Hrs   Cook Time: 10 Mins   Serves: 1

Ingredients:

- 1 1/2 cups sprite
- 2/3 cup pomegranate juice (such as POM)
- 2 tablespoons grenadine
- Maraschino cherries (for garnish)

Directions:

1. Pour sprite into an ice mold. Freeze until mostly solid, about 3 hours.
2. Add frozen sprite, pomegranate juice, and grenadine to a Ninja blender. Blend until smooth. Garnish with maraschino cherries and serve immediately.

Nutritional Value (Amount per Serving):

Calories: 497; Fat: 0.64; Carb: 124.68; Protein: 0.63

Frozen Mojitos

Prep Time: 2 Mins   Cook Time: 5 Mins   Serves: 1

Ingredients:

- 1/4 cup simple syrup
- 1/3 cup lime juice
- 1/2 cup white rum
- 1/4 cup mint leaves
- 2 cups ice

Directions:

1. Add simple syrup, lime, rum, and mint to blender. Pulse for 30 seconds to

break up the mint.

2. Add ice and blend until smooth. Pour into glasses to serve.

Nutritional Value (Amount per Serving):

Calories: 549; Fat: 13.97; Carb: 89.62; Protein: 3.24

Frozen Grasshopper

Prep Time: 10 Mins   Cook Time: 10 Mins   Serves: 1-2

Ingredients:

- 1/2 cup heavy cream
- 1/4 cup (2 ounces) aquavit (such as Krogstad)
- 1/4 cup Rich Simple Syrup
- 2 tablespoons (1 ounce) green or white crème de menthe
- 2 tablespoons (1 ounce) banana liqueur (such as Tempus Fugit Crème de Banane)
- 3 1/2 cups ice cubes

Directions:

1. Process all ingredients in the blenderuntil smooth, 1 minute to 1 minute and 30 seconds.
2. Divide grasshopper evenly between 2 chilled glasses.
3. Top evenly with grasshopper whip. Garnish with shaved chocolate, if desired.
4. Serve immediately.

Nutritional Value (Amount per Serving):

Calories: 805; Fat: 40.62; Carb: 97.06; Protein: 8.14

Boozy Frozen Strawberry Lemonade

Prep Time: 5 Mins   Cook Time: 5 Mins   Serves: 2

Ingredients:

- 1/2 cup Prosecco
- 6 tablespoons lemon-flavored vodka
- 1/4 cup loosely packed fresh basil leaves, plus more for garnish2
- 2 tablespoons limoncello
- 1 cup lemon sorbet
- 6 large fresh strawberries, hulled and halved lengthwise

Directions:

1. Using a cocktail muddler or handle of a wooden spoon, muddle together

Prosecco, vodka, basil, and limoncello in a cocktail shaker until basil is starting to bruise and tear into pieces. Set aside.

2. Process sorbet and strawberries in a Ninja blender until smooth, about 30 seconds. Pour basil infusion from cocktail shaker through a fine mesh strainer into blender; discard solids. Pulse just until combined. Transfer blended mixture to a medium-size freezer-safe bowl or resealable container. Cover and freeze until firm, at least 4 hours or up to overnight (12 hours).

3. Remove frozen mixture from freezer; let stand at room temperature until softened slightly, about 10 minutes. Scoop mixture into blender; process until smooth, about 30 seconds. Divide evenly among 4 Champagne flutes or wine glasses. Garnish with additional basil, and serve immediately.

Nutritional Value (Amount per Serving):

Calories: 45; Fat: 0.46; Carb: 12.76; Protein: 0.8

Frozen Aperol Spritzes ('Fraperol Spritzes')

Prep Time: 5 Mins   Cook Time: 8 Hrs   Serves: 1

Ingredients:

- 12 ounces Prosecco, plus more for serving
- 8 ounces Aperol
- 8 ounces water
- 1/4 cup orange liqueur, such as Cointreau
- Orange wheels, for garnish

Directions:

1. Whisk together Prosecco, Aperol, water, and orange liqueur in a pitcher. Pour mixture into 2 to 3 standard ice cube trays. Freeze until firm, at least 8 hours but preferably overnight.

2. Transfer prepared ice cubes to a Ninja blender; process until smooth and frothy. Pour into 4 wine glasses and top off with more Prosecco. Garnish with orange wheels and serve.

Nutritional Value (Amount per Serving):

Calories: 570; Fat: 13.93; Carb: 36.29; Protein: 76.47

Frozen Salted Espresso Martinis

Prep Time: 5 Mins   Cook Time: 4 Hrs   Serves: 2

Ingredients:

- 1 2/3 cups brewed espresso, at room temperature

- 6 tablespoons coffee liqueur (such as Kahlúa)
- 1/4 cup vodka
- 1 tablespoon simple syrup (see Note)
- Flaky sea salt (such as Maldon)
- 6 coffee beans

Directions:

1. Pour espresso into an ice cube tray. Freeze until solid, about 4 hours.
2. Process espresso ice cubes, coffee liqueur, vodka, and simple syrup in a Ninja blender until smooth, about 1 minute.
3. Pour evenly into 2 chilled coupe martini glasses; garnish each with a pinch of sea salt and 3 coffee beans. Serve immediately.

Nutritional Value (Amount per Serving):

Calories: 561; Fat: 30.78; Carb: 65.38; Protein: 7.14

Lassi

Prep Time: 10 Mins   Cook Time: 5 Mins   Serves: 1

Ingredients:

- 1 3/4 cups plain yogurt
- 1 1/2 cups ice water
- 6 cubes ice, crushed
- 2 tsp white sugar
- a pinch of salt

Directions:

1. Fill 6 tall glasses with ice cubes.
2. Place yogurt, ice water, crushed ice, sugar, and salt in a Ninja blender, then blend until frothy.
3. Pour over ice cubes in the glasses to serve and garnish with fresh mint if desired.

Nutritional Value (Amount per Serving):

Calories: 463; Fat: 28.77; Carb: 34.64; Protein: 17.38

Cranberry Blender Frozen Drink

Prep Time: 5 Mins   Cook Time: 5 Mins   Serves: 1

Ingredients:

- ripe banana
- peach (very ripe), peeled or 2 canned peach halves

- navel orange, peeled and sliced
- 1/2 grapefruit, peeled, sectioned and seeded
- 1 cup diced cantaloupe or 1 (10 oz.) pkg. frozen melon balls, thawed and drained
- 1 cup diced watermelon

Directions:

1. Pour cranberry juice and one of the fruits into blender with crushed ice cubes. Whirl until smooth.
2. Add superfine sugar to taste. Pour into a tall glass.

Nutritional Value (Amount per Serving):

Calories: 965; Fat: 3.37; Carb: 249.89; Protein: 10.78

Banana-berry Drink

Prep Time: 5 Mins   Cook Time: 5 Mins   Serves: 2

Ingredients:

- 1 ripe med. Banana
- 1 c. milk
- 1/2 c. strawberry yogurt
- 4 ice cubes

Directions:

1. Remove the peel from the banana.
2. Use the table knife to cut the banana into chunks.
3. In the blender container put milk, yogurt, ice cubes and banana.
4. Blend about 1/2 minute or until smooth.
5. Turn the blender off.
6. Pour the drink into the glasses.
7. Serve with strawberries, if you like.

Nutritional Value (Amount per Serving):

Calories: 339; Fat: 10.26; Carb: 59.71; Protein: 7.37

Uncompearable Frozen Cocktail

Prep Time: 5 Mins   Cook Time: 5 Mins   Serves: 2

Ingredients:

- 1/2 cup, plus 2 tablespoons canned fruit cocktail in heavy syrup, puréed (from 15- ounce can)
- juice of 2 fresh limes

- 3 ounces (1/4 cup, plus 2 tablespoons) pear-flavored premium vodka
- 2 tablespoons sugar
- Ice
- pineapple wedges and cherries, for garnish

Directions:

1. Purée fruit cocktail in blender.
2. Transfer purée to a separate bowl/pitcher.
3. Rinse blender and return to the base.
4. Add lime juice, vodka and fruit cocktail purée to blender. Add sugar.
5. Fill serving glass with ice, pour ice into blender and repeat adding another glass of ice.
6. Blend well. Pour into cocktail glasses.
7. Garnish with a pineapple wedge and a cherry.

Nutritional Value (Amount per Serving):

Calories: 176; Fat: 3.58; Carb: 37.75; Protein: 1.23

Chapter 7: Dessert Smoothies

Homemade Ice Cream Recipe

Prep Time: 2 Mins   Cook Time: 3 Mins   Serves: 1

Ingredients:

- 10 ounces frozen berries, or any other frozen fruit
- 2 tablespoons granulated sweetener, optional
- 2/3 cup heavy cream

Directions:

1. Place frozen berries and sweetener, if using, in a Ninja blender; process or pulse just until the fruit is roughly chopped.
2. Pour in the heavy cream, and continue to process just until everything is incorporated and smooth. Add more heavy cream if the mixture is too thick. Scrape down the sides with a spatula as needed.
3. Serve immediately or freeze for later.

Nutritional Value (Amount per Serving):

Calories: 570; Fat: 30.07; Carb: 76.85; Protein: 2.78

Orange Ice Cream (Quick and Easy Blender Recipe!)

Prep Time: 10 Mins   Cook Time: 7 Hrs   Serves: 2

Ingredients:

- 1 1/2 cups heavy whipping cream
- 1/2 cup + 1 Tbsp whole milk
- 1/3 cup sugar
- a little less than 1 cup orange juice
- 4 Tbsp grated orange zest (organic)

Directions:

1. Pour the cream and milk into the blender container with the sugar. Then add the orange juice and zest and blend for about 45 seconds or until it's well mixed.
2. Pour into a metal pan and place in the freezer for about an hour.
3. Remove from the freezer and stir with a spoon. Repeat this two more times (twice in two hours.)
4. You'll see the mixture begin to take on the texture of ice cream. When it's ready, scoop into glasses, cups, or cones to serve.

Nutritional Value (Amount per Serving):

Calories: 496; Fat: 35.33; Carb: 42.8; Protein: 4.72

Blender Creamsicle Ice Cream Sodas

Prep Time: 5 Mins   Cook Time: 5 Mins   Serves: 2

Ingredients:

- 1/2 cup orange juice
- 1/2 cup soda water or seltzer water
- 1 1/2 cups light or fat free vanilla ice cream
- 1/2 cup ice cubes

Directions:

1. Add all ingredients in a Ninja blender.
2. Process and blend until creamy.
3. Pour into glasses and serve.

Nutritional Value (Amount per Serving):

Calories: 352; Fat: 15.72; Carb: 44.13; Protein: 8.73

Chocolate Chia Pudding Mousse

Prep Time: 5 Mins   Cook Time: 4 Hrs   Serves: 2

Ingredients:

- 2 cup dairy-free milk
- 1/2 cup chia seeds
- 1/4 cup cacao powder , or cocoa powder
- 1/4 cup maple syrup
- 2 tsp vanilla extract

Directions:

1. Add all of the ingredients to a Ninja blender.
2. Blend for a minute, or until the pudding is creamy.
3. Transfer the pudding to a bowl, cover and chill at least 4 hours.
4. Serve the chocolate chia mousse with a dollop of coconut whipped cream, chocolate shavings, and chopped nuts.

Nutritional Value (Amount per Serving):

Calories: 456; Fat: 14.9; Carb: 70.73; Protein: 16.37

Healthy Blueberry Blender Ice Cream

Prep Time: 5 Mins   Cook Time: 5 Mins   Serves: 2

Ingredients:

- 2 Frozen Bananas, Cut into chunks
- 8 Ounces Yogurt
- 1 Cup Frozen Blueberries

Directions:

1. Place all ingredients into the bowl of a Ninja blender.
2. Pulse until well combined and creamy.
3. Serve immediately with any desired toppings.

Nutritional Value (Amount per Serving):

Calories: 452; Fat: 2.75; Carb: 101.79; Protein: 15.77

Disney Dole Whip Recipe

Prep Time: 5 Mins   Cook Time: 5 Mins   Serves: 1

Ingredients:

- 1 scoop of vanilla ice cream
- 4 ounces of pineapple juice
- 2 cups of frozen pineapple

Directions:

1. Add all 3 ingredients to a Ninja blender, and blend until smooth.
2. You can eat it as is or squeeze it out from a piping bag to form that iconic yellow swirl. A Ziploc bag or parchment paper work as well.
3. Top with a cocktail umbrella for some tropical fun.

Nutritional Value (Amount per Serving):

Calories: 516; Fat: 1.01; Carb: 132.21; Protein: 3.05

Paleo & Vegan Pistachio Ice Cream (Only 4 Ingredients!)

Prep Time: 5 Mins   Cook Time: 2 Hrs 30 Mins   Serves: 2

Ingredients:

- 2 1/2 cup full-fat coconut milk
- 3/4 cup shelled pistachios unsalted
- 1/4 cup maple syrup plus more to taste
- 1/2 tsp almond extract
- Optional: Chopped pistachios for garnish

Directions:

1. Combine coconut milk and pistachios in a Ninja blender and blend until smooth and creamy.
2. Add maple syrup and almond extract, and blend together.
3. Taste and add more maple syrup if you want it sweeter. It'll taste less sweet once frozen.
4. Pour the mixture into an ice cream maker and churn following the manufacturer's directions. The mixture should firm up and turn into a ball after about 20-30 minutes. Transfer to an airtight container and freeze for at least 2 hours.
5. Serve in a bowl or cone (these are gluten free), sprinkled with chopped pistachios.

Nutritional Value (Amount per Serving):

Calories: 1075; Fat: 94.39; Carb: 56.85; Protein: 17.08

Vanilla Milkshake Without Ice Cream

Prep Time: 5 Mins   Cook Time: 5 Mins   Serves: 1-2

Ingredients:

- 15 ice cubes
- 2 cups milk
- 1/2 cup sugar
- 1 pinch vanilla extract

Directions:

1. Blend ice cubes, milk, sugar, and vanilla extract until smooth.
2. Pour in glasses. Enjoy!

Nutritional Value (Amount per Serving):

Calories: 409; Fat: 18.69; Carb: 42.17; Protein: 11.67

Raspberry Yogurt Dessert Smoothie

Prep Time: 5 Mins   Cook Time: 5 Mins   Serves: 1

Ingredients:

- 1 frozen banana
- 3/4 cup frozen raspberries
- 3/4 cup chocolate unsweetened almond milk
- 3/4 cup greek yogurt

Directions:

1. Blend all of the ingredients and add your favorite toppings (coconut,

chocolate chips, almond slivers, goji berries, chia seeds, etc)
Nutritional Value (Amount per Serving):

Calories: 1393; Fat: 51.57; Carb: 215.67; Protein: 31.7

Peach Yogurt Dessert Smoothie

Prep Time: 5 Mins   Cook Time: 5 Mins   Serves: 1

Ingredients:

- 2 cups Greek yogurt
- 2 peaches; divided
- Sweetener of your choice optional

Directions:

1. Wash and roughly chop one of the peaches and slice the second peach.
2. Using a Ninja blender, blend yogurt, chopped peach and sweetener, if using.
3. Divide into 2-3 serving bowls, garnish with your favorite toppings (I used peach slices, granola, sliced almonds, crushed pistachios and mint leaves).
4. Serve immediately.

Nutritional Value (Amount per Serving):

Calories: 598; Fat: 1.69; Carb: 125.23; Protein: 31.26

Superfood Green Dessert Smoothie Recipe

Prep Time: 4 Mins   Cook Time: 5 Mins   Serves: 2

Ingredients:

- 1/2 cup milk or almond milk
- 1/2 cup ice
- 2 tablespoons fresh lemon juice
- 2 frozen bananas
- 1/4 avocado
- 2 handfuls spinach
- 1 handful kale

Directions:

1. Add the smoothie base ingredients to a blender and blend until smooth. Divide into two bowls and top with remaining ingredients.

Nutritional Value (Amount per Serving):

Calories: 762; Fat: 30.56; Carb: 125.94; Protein: 10.68

Vegan Spinach Ginger Dessert Smoothie

Prep Time: 10 Mins   Cook Time: 5 Mins   Serves: 2

Ingredients:

- 2 1/2 cups Spinach Baby
- 1/2 inch Ginger
- 1 Banana large
- 1/2 cup Oats
- 1 tablespoon Maple Syrup
- 1 cup Coconut Milk thick unsweetened

Directions:

1. Blend everything (spinach, ginger, banana, oats, maple syrup and coconut milk) along with a few cubes of ice (5-6) in a Ninja blender till smooth.
2. Chill for half an hour in the refrigerator if you don't have ice because smoothie bowls are fantastic when cold.
3. Serve in bowls topped with your favorite fruits, seeds and nuts. Consume within the hour.

Nutritional Value (Amount per Serving):

Calories: 542; Fat: 31.32; Carb: 74.5; Protein: 9.84

Mango Dessert Smoothie

Prep Time: 10 Mins   Cook Time: 5 Mins   Serves: 1

Ingredients:

- 1 cup Mango frozen chunks
- 1 Banana frozen
- 1 cup Orange Juice

Directions:

1. Place the mango, banana and orange juice into a Ninja blender and blend until smooth.
2. If you want to add more liquid for a thinner smoothie, you can add more orange juice, or water.

Nutritional Value (Amount per Serving):

Calories: 679; Fat: 2.35; Carb: 171.4; Protein: 6.56

Chapter 8: Dressing & Sauces

Lemon Tahini Sauce

Prep Time: 5 Mins   Cook Time: 5 Mins   Serves: 2

Ingredients:

- 1/4 cup tahini
- 2 tablespoons lemon juice
- 2 tablespoons water
- 1 tablespoon low sodium soy sauce
- 1/2 piece fresh ginger
- 1/2 teapoons garlic powder
- 1 teaspoon hot sauce of your choice

Directions:

1. Blend all of your ingredients in a Ninja blender or food processor until smooth, and you're good to go.

Nutritional Value (Amount per Serving):

Calories: 202; Fat: 16.25; Carb: 11.32; Protein: 6.5

Spicy Tahini Dressing Recipe

Prep Time: 10 Mins   Cook Time: 5 Mins   Serves: 2

Ingredients:

- 2 cloves of garlic
- 1 piece fresh ginger
- 2-3 teaspoons chili-garlic sauce
- 3/4 cup water
- 3/4 cups tahini
- 1 tablespoon agave nectar - optional, or to taste (see note above)
- 1 tablespoon low-sodium soy sauce
- juice of 1 fresh lime

Directions:

1. Combine all of your ingredients in your blender, and puree until smooth. If needed, add more water by the tablespoon to reach your desired thickness.

Nutritional Value (Amount per Serving):

Calories: 569; Fat: 49.5; Carb: 24.34; Protein: 16.71

Cashew Cream Sauce Recipe

Prep Time: 15 Mins   Cook Time: 5 Mins   Serves: 2

Ingredients:

- 1 cup cashews - soaked in hot water for 10-15 minutes, then drained (see note)
- 1/2 cup water - NOT the soaking water
- 3 cloves garlic
- 2 tablespoons lemon juice
- salt and pepper - to taste

Directions:

1. Combine all of the cashew cream ingredients in your Ninja blender, and puree until smooth.
2. Season to taste with salt and pepper.

Nutritional Value (Amount per Serving):

Calories: 19; Fat: 0.1; Carb: 4.67; Protein: 0.79

Cashew Queso Recipe

Prep Time: 15 Mins   Cook Time: 5 Mins   Serves: 2

Ingredients:

- 1 cup cashews - soaked in hot water for 10-15 minutes
- 1/2 cup salsa - Choose your favorite!
- 1 tablespoon apple cider vinegar
- 2 tablespoons olive oil
- 1/4 cup nutritional yeast
- 2 cloves garlic

Directions:

1. Toss all of the ingredients into the blender, and puree until smooth.
2. Then, blend for a little bit longer.

Nutritional Value (Amount per Serving):

Calories: 213; Fat: 13.96; Carb: 13.59; Protein: 9.8

Tahini Ranch Dressing Recipe

Prep Time: 5 Mins   Cook Time: 5 Mins   Serves: 1-2

Ingredients:

- 3/4 cup tahini
- 1 tablespoon dried dill
- 2 teaspoons garlic powder
- 2 teaspoons onion powder
- 1 cup water - or more, as needed, to reach your desired consistency - How much you need will depend on the tahini you're using.
- 1/2 cup lemon juice
- 1 teaspoon sea salt
- 1/2 teaspoon black pepper

Directions:

1. Combine all of the ingredients in your Ninja blender, and puree until smooth.
2. Add water one tablespoons as a time, if you want to thin the dressing out any more.

Nutritional Value (Amount per Serving):

Calories: 579; Fat: 49.08; Carb: 29.73; Protein: 16.88

Citrus Salad Dressing Recipe

Prep Time: 5 Mins   Cook Time: 5 Mins   Serves: 1

Ingredients:

- 2 tablespoons lemon juice - fresh squeezed or bottled is fine
- 1/4 cup orange juice - fresh squeezed or bottled is fine
- 1/4 cup olive oil
- 1 tablespoon maple syrup
- 1 clove garlic
- 1/4 teaspoon salt - or more, to taste

Directions:

1. Combine all of the vinaigrette ingredients in your Ninja blender, and blend until completely smooth.
2. Chill until ready to serve.

Nutritional Value (Amount per Serving):

Calories: 571; Fat: 54.19; Carb: 23.53; Protein: 0.74

No-Cook Miso Gravy Sauce Recipe

Prep Time: 5 Mins   Cook Time: 5 Mins   Serves: 1

Ingredients:

- 1/4 cup red miso paste
- 1/2 cup room temperature water
- 2 tablespoons olive oil
- 1 medium shallot - cut into quarters
- 2 cloves garlic
- 1/4 cup nutritional yeast

Directions:

1. Put all of the ingredients into your Ninja blender, and puree until smooth.
2. If it isn't at the thickness you want, add more nutritional yeast to thicken or water to thin. If you overdo it on the water and things start to taste a bit diluted, add miso, a teaspoon at a time, to bump the flavor back up.

Nutritional Value (Amount per Serving):

Calories: 525; Fat: 31.82; Carb: 36.58; Protein: 25.87

Cranberry Vinaigrette Recipe

Prep Time: 5 Mins   Cook Time: 5 Mins   Serves: 1

Ingredients:

- 1 cup fresh cranberries
- 1/2 cup olive oil
- 2 tablespoon balsamic vinegar
- 1 tablespoon chopped ginger - no need to peel
- 2 tablespoons maple syrup

Directions:

1. Combine all of the ingredients in your Ninja blender, and blend until smooth.
2. Season to taste with salt and pepper, and pour it onto all of the salads!

Nutritional Value (Amount per Serving):

Calories: 1228; Fat: 108.32; Carb: 67.54; Protein: 0.28

Vegan Red Pepper Sauce

Prep Time: 10 Mins   Cook Time: 8 Mins   Serves: 1

Ingredients:

- 6-8 ounces fettuccini
- 6 cups baby spinach - or other quick-wilting greens
- 1 12 ounce jar roasted red peppers - drained

- 3/4 cup packed fresh basil leaves and stems
- 1/2 cup cashews, walnuts, almonds, or pine nuts - Use pumpkin seeds for nut-free.
- 1/2 cup olive oil
- 2-4 cloves garlic - depending on size. Use 2 cloves if they're large, 4 if they're small.
- 1-2 tablespoons red wine vinegar - to taste
- 1 tablespoon nutritional yeast - optional

Directions:

1. Combine all of the sauce ingredients (start with 1 tablespoon of the vinegar) in your Ninja blender and run it until you have an even mixture. You can go for a chunkier pesto, like I did, or keep running until it's smooth and creamy.
2. Season to taste with salt and pepper, and add the second tablespoon of vinegar, if you want it more tangy.

Nutritional Value (Amount per Serving):

Calories: 1690; Fat: 158.98; Carb: 50.45; Protein: 31.16

Creamy Strawberry Salad Dressing

Prep Time: 5 Mins   Cook Time: 5 Mins   Serves: 1-2

Ingredients:

- 1 cup strawberries - stems removed
- 2 tablespoons agave nectar
- 1/3 cup apple cider vinegar
- 1/3 cup sunflower oil
- 1/4 cup basil leaves - loosely packed
- 1 teaspoon salt
- 1/4 teaspoon black pepper

Directions:

1. Combine all of the dressing ingredients in your Ninja blender, and blend until smooth.

Nutritional Value (Amount per Serving):

Calories: 370; Fat: 36.25; Carb: 12.68; Protein: 0.64

Vegan Cacio e Pepe Dressing

Prep Time: 15 Mins   Cook Time: 10 Mins   Serves: 1

Ingredients:

- 1/2 cup cashews
- 1/3 cup water
- 4 to 5 teaspoons lemon juice
- 1 tablespoon nutritional yeast
- 1 teaspoon black pepper
- 3/4 teaspoon sea salt
- 8 ounces spaghetti - or long, skinny pasta of choice, or use zoodles

Directions:

1. Pour enough boiling water over the cashews to cover, and let them sit for 15 minutes. Drain.
2. While the cashews soak, cook your pasta according to package directions or spiralize your zucchini, whichever you're doing!
3. Throw the cashews, water, lemon, nutritional yeast, pepper, and salt into your Ninja blender, and puree until very smooth. Just keep blending, scraping down the sides of the blender as needed, until you get a smooth salt and pepper cashew cream. Taste and adjust seasoning, blending between additions.
4. Toss the sauce with the noodles or zoodles, coating evenly. Taste, and add more salt and pepper, if you like. Serve immediately.

Nutritional Value (Amount per Serving):

Calories: 953; Fat: 51.26; Carb: 101.36; Protein: 37.42

Vegan Avocado sauce

Prep Time: 10 Mins   Cook Time: 5 Mins   Serves: 1-2

Ingredients:

- 1 Haas avocado
- 1 cup fresh basil leaves - loosely packed
- 1/2 cup water - plus more, if needed, to reach your desired consistency
- 2 cloves garlic
- 2 tablespoons cashews - raw or roasted is fine, or you can use pine nuts
- 1/4 cup lemon juice
- 2 tablespoons nutritional yeast - optional
- salt and black pepper - to taste

Directions:

1. Put all of your avocado sauce ingredients into the Ninja blender, and blend until smooth. You can add water 1 tablespoon at a time, as needed, to get things moving.

2. Adjust the salt and pepper, if necessary.

Nutritional Value (Amount per Serving):

Calories: 215; Fat: 15.13; Carb: 17.5; Protein: 7.08

An Exceptional Ginger Carrot Dressing

Prep Time: 5 Mins   Cook Time:5 Mins   Serves: 1

Ingredients:

- 1/3 cup full-fat coconut milk
- 1/4 teaspoon ground turmeric, or more to taste
- 5 tablespoons peeled ginger, chopped to measure
- 3 medium farmers' market carrots, scrubbed
- 1/2 of a serrano pepper, stemmed, or to taste
- 1/3 cup extra virgin olive oil
- 1/2 teaspoon fine grain sea salt
- 2 tablespoons toasted sesame oil
- 1 tablespoon miso (optional)
- 1 tablespoon maple syrup
- 1/4 cup / 60 ml brown rice vinegar
- 4 small shallots, peeled (or less if your shallots are strong)

Directions:

1. Blend the coconut milk, turmeric, ginger, carrots, pepper, olive oil, salt, toasted sesame oil, miso, maple syrup, brown rice vinegar, and shallots in a Ninja blender until very smooth.
2. Taste, and adjust, if needed, with more salt or vinegar, or any other ingredient you think might give a little boost.

Nutritional Value (Amount per Serving):

Calories: 1156; Fat: 80.21; Carb: 103.44; Protein: 12.79

Creamy Cashew Green Goddess Dressing

Prep Time: 5 Mins   Cook Time: 5 Mins   Serves: 1-2

Ingredients:

- 1/2 cup (75 g) raw cashews (covered in boiling water and soaked 1-8 hours)
- 1/3 cup (80 ml) packed basil leaves
- 1/3 cup (80 ml) chopped chives
- 1/4 cup (60 ml) packed tarragon leaves
- 1 large garlic clove, peeled

- 2 teaspoons (10 ml) drained capers
- 3 tablespoons (45 ml) fresh lemon juice (more to taste)
- 1 tablespoon (15 ml) extra-virgin olive oil
- 1/4 teaspoon salt (more to taste)
- 1/4 cup (60 ml) ice water, plus more as needed

Directions:

1. In the bowl of the Ninja blender, combine the soaked and drained cashews, basil, chives, tarragon, garlic, capers, lemon juice, olive oil, salt, and 1/4 cup ice water.
2. Blend, until the dressing is creamy-smooth, adding more ice water as needed until you like the consistency.
3. Taste, adding more lemon or salt if you like. Refrigerate airtight for up to 1 week.

Nutritional Value (Amount per Serving):

Calories: 124; Fat: 6.44; Carb: 15.01; Protein: 2.56

Five Minute Avocado Cilantro Dressing

Prep Time: 5 Mins   Cook Time: 5 Mins   Serves: 2

Ingredients:

- half an avocado
- 1/4 cup Greek yogurt
- 1/2 cup water (more as needed to adjust consistency)
- 1 cup cilantro leaves and stems
- 1 small clove of garlic
- 1/2 teaspoon salt
- a squeeze of lime juice

Directions:

1. Pulse all ingredients in a Ninja blender until smooth.
2. Voila! Avocado Cilantro Dressing!

Nutritional Value (Amount per Serving):

Calories: 107; Fat: 7.54; Carb: 7.95; Protein: 4.25

Mango Cilantro Salad Dressing

Prep Time: 10 Mins   Cook Time: 5 Mins   Serves: 1

Ingredients:

- 1 cup Ripe Mangoes diced

- 1/2 cup Cilantro / Coriander leaves
- 1 Thai Red Chili
- 3 Garlic Cloves
- 2 tablespoons Red Wine Vinegar
- 3/4 teaspoon Salt
- 1/2 cup Olive Oil Extra Virgin

Directions:

1. Add mangoes, cilantro, red chili, garlic, red wine vinegar and salt to the Ninja blender. Start blending and once the ingredients start breaking down, slowly pour in olive oil till the dressing emulsifies and becomes creamy.

Nutritional Value (Amount per Serving):

Calories: 619; Fat: 51.17; Carb: 42.18; Protein: 6.36

Vegan Sauce

Prep Time: 10 Mins   Cook Time: 20 Mins   Serves: 2

Ingredients:

- 1/2 cup (75 grams) raw cashews
- 1/2 cup (56g grams) almond flour, or more cashews
- 1/3 cup (20 grams) nutritional yeast, increase to half a cup for a more pronounced cheesy flavor
- 1 cup (240 mls) plant milk, unsweetened & unflavored
- 1 clove garlic
- 1 teaspoon sea salt
- 1 teaspoon freshly ground black pepper

Directions:

1. Cover the cashew nuts with boiling water from a kettle and leave to soak for 15 minutes.
2. Drain the cashews, then add them and all of the other sauce ingredients to the Ninja blender. Blend until completely smooth.

Nutritional Value (Amount per Serving):

Calories: 952; Fat: 72.2; Carb: 54.84; Protein: 32.8

Chipotle Sauce

Prep Time: 5 Mins   Cook Time: 10 Mins   Serves: 1

Ingredients:

- 1 tablespoon extra-virgin olive oil
- 1/2 sweet onion, chopped
- 2 garlic cloves, minced
- 1 teaspoon ground cumin
- 1 28- ounce can whole, peeled tomatoes
- 1-3 chipotle peppers from a can in adobo sauce, start with one, add more to taste
- kosher salt & freshly ground black pepper, to taste

Directions:

1. Preheat a large skillet over medium heat. Add onions and cook, stirring occasionally, until soft and translucent, about five minutes. Add garlic and ground cumin, cook another 2 minutes, stirring frequently (turn down heat if garlic starts to brown).
2. Place onion mixture along with tomatoes and peppers into the Ninja blender; blend until very smooth.

Nutritional Value (Amount per Serving):

Calories: 200; Fat: 9.46; Carb: 25.01; Protein: 6.49

APPENDIX RECIPE INDEX

Made in the USA
Las Vegas, NV
23 November 2024

12502588R00057